ON THE PHILOSOPHY OF EDUCATION

Towards an Anthroposophical View

DANIELE-HADI IRANDOOST

978-0-6452126-5-5
On the Philosophy of Education:
Towards an Anthroposophical View
Daniele-Hadi Irandoost

© Manticore Press, Melbourne, Australia, 2022.

All rights reserved, no section of this book may be utilized without permission, except brief quotations, including electronic reproductions without the permission of the copyright holders and publisher. Published in Australia.

Thema Classification: JNA (Philosophy of Education), JNB (History of Education), JNC (Psychology of Education), QRYC5 (Anthroposophy), JPFB (Anarchism), QDX (Popular Philosophy).

MANTICORE PRESS
WWW.MANTICORE.PRESS

CONTENTS

INTRODUCTION 7

SECTION I
EDUCATION IN ANARCHISM, LANGUAGE, PSYCHOANALYSIS, AND RIGHTS

CHAPTER I 13
THE PHILOSOPHY OF ANARCHIST ALTERNATIVES TO NATIONAL EDUCATION
- Part I: Anarchism 15
- Part II: Anarchist Education 20
- Part III: Counterarguments 25
- Conclusion 29
- Bibliography 31

CHAPTER II 33
ON LANGUAGE AND THE 'EXTENDED-MIND' THEORY
- Part I: The 'Extended-Mind' and Language 34
- Part II: The Communicative Conception of Language 39
- Part III: Wittgenstein, Language, and Thought 44
- Conclusion 48
- Bibliography 51

CHAPTER III 53
FROM THE COUCH TO THE CLASSROOM
- Part I: 'Mediating Texts' as a Psychoanalytic Technique 55
- Part II: Freudian Psychoanalysis and the 'Death Drive' 57
- Part III: Assessing 'Mediating Texts' — Its Theory and Practice .. 60

Conclusion 65

Bibliography 67

CHAPTER IV 69
OF THE RIGHT OF PRISONERS TO EDUCATION

Part I: 'Utility' of Schooling Prisoners 70

Part II: Kantian Ethics on the Right of Prisoners to Education 74

Part III: Foucault, Power, and Prisons 79

Conclusion 82

Bibliography 85

SECTION II

ON SOPHIE, JEAN-JACQUES ROUSSEAU, AND WOMEN'S EDUCATION

INITIAL THOUGHTS 91

CHAPTER I 95
OF ROUSSEAU

Part I: Progress, Inequality, and Human Nature 96

Part II: Religion and Politics 102

Conclusion 107

CHAPTER II 109
ON EMILE

Part I: Personal Development 110

Part II: Social Development 116

Conclusion 120

CHAPTER III 123
CRITIQUING SOPHIE'S EDUCATION

Part I: Sophie's Education 124

Part II: Received Criticisms 128
Conclusion 135

CHAPTER IV 137
A DEFENCE OF ROUSSEAU

Part I: Sophie's Superiority 138
Part II: Sophie and Emile as Equals 142
Conclusion 149

FINAL THOUGHTS 151
SECTION II BIBLIOGRAPHY 155
AFTERWORD BY DAVID WILLIAM PARRY 161
ACKNOWLEDGEMENTS 167

APPENDIX 169
METHODOLOGICAL CRITIQUE OF SKINNER'S BEHAVIOUR 'SCIENCE'

Part I: Behaviourism and Skinner 170
Part II: A Methodological Weakness 171
Part III: Redeeming Behaviourism and Skinner 172
Conclusion 172
Bibliography 175

INTRODUCTION

The Philosophy of Education, as an academic discipline, emerged in the 20th century, primarily in anglophone universities. Of course, the Philosophy of Education refers to the study of education by philosophers, while its aim as an abstract field is to examine the goals, forms, methods, and meaning of education. Hence, it is concerned with both fundamental philosophical analyses as well as specific pedagogical practices; pedagogy, briefly, is the theory and practice of interactions that take place between a learner and a teacher, not to mention learning processes and how these are influenced by social, political and psychological developments society-wide. Be that as it may, intellectual accounts of philosophy of education (note, lower-case lettering) are easily found in ancient texts, the earliest probably being Plato's *Republic,* authored around 375 BC, even though there appears to have existed an intervening era between the Athenian philosopher and later thoughts developed during the Renaissance, Reformation, and Age of Enlightenment in the West; albeit, it is worth noting that, outside the West, the philosophy of education was described even before Plato, notably by Confucius in 551–479 BCE.

Nonetheless, before I continue any further, I believe it is important to mention some contextual details regarding this book. Firstly, the volume of papers gathered herein grew out of my third postgraduate studies at UCL Institute of Education during an MA Philosophy of Education and PGCE (teacher training qualification) in History at Aberystwyth University, Wales. Remarkably, the

Institute of Education has been ranked first in the world of education in the QS World University Rankings since 2014, while as the largest education research body in the United Kingdom, it specialises in postgraduate study of education and has over 100 research projects at any one time funded by external agencies, including government departments. All in all, it is composed of an impressive array of international students and houses the world's first Confucius Institute for Schools, supporting the teaching and learning of Mandarin Chinese in schools. Certainly, with that in mind, the course I undertook there is perhaps unique to this institution.

Secondly, it is vital to emphasise the fact that education is no less important than other disciplines in philosophy, including aesthetics, epistemology, ethics, logic, metaphysics, and philosophy of mind. After all, among the most important issues faced by any country in the world is the state of its education, apart from its health care system, immigration, crime, economy, security, and environment. Certainly, each manifesto plan by the governing parties in Great Britain usually refers to some aspect of education as a national matter. International reports by non-governmental bodies also publish indexes ranking the education system of each country — regardless of whatever these are supposed to represent, in practice. However, this is not to say education aims to enlighten citizens of each nation. By contrast, some argue (as demonstrated in the fourth chapter), education may be used as a 'weapon' by political elites to shape public opinion and knowledge.

Thirdly, the intended audience of this text consists of those not only interested in an introduction to this remarkably exceptional field, but also specialists who undertake to delve deeply into the subjects discussed. Hence, whereas students of philosophy will benefit from gaining insights into key ancient and contemporary thinkers — for instance, Rousseau, Kant, Foucault, and Andy Clark — a beginner will enter our anglophone discourses from wider perspectives found in anarchism, language, psychology, rights, and feminism, to name a few. As such, the style in which each chapter is written is concise and to the point. No doubt, several concepts may be complex to understand. In these instances, I personally recommend that the reader perseveres and continues the process of learning.

With that said, it must be borne in mind that philosophy is ultimately merely one form of creativity. Philosophy is undoubtedly a crucial embodiment of rational thought, yet, it does not always provide answers to our most demanding dilemmas as human beings. In which case, as Kierkegaard discovered, art and, above all, theology must begin after philosophy, since, at the end of the day, too much 'scientific' thinking sometimes results in little creativity or imagination. Hence, my own conclusion is that perhaps our thoughts on education systems worldwide should benefit from unconventional and alternative ways of thinking. As Rudolf Steiner said,

> Our highest endeavour must be to develop free human beings who are able of themselves to impart purpose and direction to their lives. The need for imagination, a sense of truth, and a feeling of responsibility — these three forces are the very nerve of education.

This is an anthroposophical ideal I would like to uphold for the entirety of this publication.

SECTION I

EDUCATION IN ANARCHISM, LANGUAGE,
PSYCHOANALYSIS, AND RIGHTS

I. THE PHILOSOPHY OF ANARCHIST ALTERNATIVES TO NATIONAL EDUCATION

> I went to the Rudolf Steiner School in New York, and you're not allowed to watch TV.
> — *Jennifer Aniston, American Actress*

Few political ideologies receive as vehemently bad press as anarchism. Upon hearing the word, unread members of the public assumingly envisage sabotage, political assassination, vandalism, and violent protest: in basic terms, anything that might proceed from disorganised, and somewhat messy, political action. Admittedly, that being the case, one must not rashly claim that these things *are* indistinguishable from the history of anarchism; for, as it happens, some sectors within anarchist thought do, in fact, promote that romantic idea of violence for the achievement of total freedom and independence (see, for example, Malatesta, 1894). Be that as it may, anarchism, as it was conceived by its most important forerunner, William Godwin, rebuked all violent behaviour absolutely, contending instead for a peaceful transition into a stateless society (Kramnick, 1985: 38ff.); an advocacy clearly supported by the likes of other anarchists, such as Henry David Thoreau and Leo Tolstoy.

Of course, it must always be borne in mind that central to the anarchist ideal is a society free from any type of political authority:

all humankind being free-thinking, rational creatures, requiring no external governance, and instead relying on that of their own internal judgment alone (Godwin, 1985: 75-78). One cannot help stress, on this account, anarchists have a deep-rooted distrust of not only the state itself, but of every authority established and reinforced by the hierarchical structures of the state (McLaughlin, 2007: 12f.). The police, courts, military, and Church are all corrupting influences that must be abolished no matter what. Even school — as run by the state — does not escape denouncement: 'The project of a national education ought uniformly to be discouraged on account of its obvious alliance with national government [...] Before we put so powerful a machine under the direction of so ambiguous an agent, it behoves us to consider well what it is that we do', Godwin (1985: 616-617) declared in his celebrated *Enquiry Concerning Political Justice*, the 'sacred text' (Kramnick, 1985: 7) on anarchist principles.

As a radical sentiment in itself, no doubt, it would be hardly surprising if such a statement were to be rejected at once — especially if one is mindful of education's interwoven history with government, not to mention the given 'ascendency' of liberalism and the liberal state in the West today (Suissa, 2010: 19). Nonetheless, ideas of this sort cannot simply be cast aside if we intend to resolve political and, so to speak, social problems of the day. In which case, the aim of this chapter is to discuss anarchist alternatives to national education through a philosophy-oriented perspective. Divided into three sections, the first sets out an all-round sketch of the politics and philosophy of anarchism, namely its critiques of government and an image of the anarchist dream or (for that matter) values; focusing, in particular, on the ideas of William Godwin as our starting point. The second section, next, details the anarchist view on education as well as national education. And the final part lays down the most significant shortcomings of anarchism, generally and education-wise, at both theoretical and practical levels. By the end of this inquiry, three findings are observed altogether. First, despite the fact William Godwin is mentioned within the literature on anarchist education, he is often overshadowed by social anarchists, even though his ideas effectively run through the whole of anarchist thought. Second, a fresh review of Edmund Burke's thoughts on human nature and the significance of tradition appears necessary for a nuanced interpretation of the anarchist outcome. Third, historical facts seem to indicate evidence of anarchism's and, in particular, anarchist education's practical conceivability at this point in time — notwithstanding the many charges of utopianism from naysayers. It is concluded, a great task lies ahead, but that gradual direct action is significant under the current political and social circumstances if there is to be any progress and improvement toward the anarchist dream.

Part I: Anarchism

No discussion of anarchism can be complete without an understanding of its basic principles and original context. This is an intellectual instance which (before investigating others) allows William Godwin as the so-called modern 'prophet' of anarchist thought (Kramnick, 1985: 7) to forward this viewpoint as a perfect starting point for deliberation. Godwin (1756–1836), of course, was an English political philosopher in the Age of Reason or Enlightenment. Under this movement, essentially, Godwin and his contemporaries (like Locke, Montesquieu, and Rousseau) believed not simply in the theory of 'original sin', but in the feasibility either of humans' natural goodness or, alternatively, the effect of external circumstances above all other things (as detailed below). Having emerged out of the Age of Faith, when kings held unquestionable divine power, the philosophers of this modern era questioned not just the existence of God, in its traditional sense of the word, but also, in point of fact, the relevance of religious institutions altogether. Instead, convinced by a different worldview, the new philosophers championed the power of reason as the ultimate good. To this effect, liberal values, like truth, toleration, freedom, and individualism (as they were perceived back then) began to take precedence; all leading, as it happened, to staggering political and social transformations in Western Europe, pinnacling in various forms, most importantly of all, the French Revolution. Obviously, though not everyone agreed on the specifics of these changes, there was nevertheless near-unanimous support — amongst these progressive theorists — for a shift in political power away from monarchs to the people, as democracy gained momentum.

No matter how familiar these facts may be to us, broadly, this was the basic background within which anarchist principles were assembled. The only difference being, excepting Godwin, these thinkers did not take Enlightenment values to their radical extreme. Surprisingly, in accordance, it was only Godwin — amid the aforementioned — who opposed any type of authority or 'monopoly' restraining individual freedom or thought: including the institutions of government, God, and even marriage. That being noted, overall, Godwin's conclusions may ultimately come down to two overarching points: on the one hand, the good of individual rationality, and, on the other, the evil of authority (as used interchangeably with power or monopoly). He believed, in a way, all individuals are equally capable of reason, while authority, as imposed, especially by governments and their institutions, remains the foremost impediment to this unique development.

Assuredly, to be more specific on this matter, Godwin attested that if individuals were given the freedom to inquire rationally, they would — precisely because of their faculty to reason — be able to resolve any problems without needing the supervision of a higher body. Crime, injustice, inequality, and all other 'evils', essentially, would be worked out by individuals on their own free 'volition' (Godwin, 1985: 335ff.). One should recall at this point, Godwin, as a philosopher of the Age of Reason, believed in the existence of absolute 'Truth', one which could only be discovered through reason alone. In this regard, he especially emphasised the importance of 'perfectibility' (ibid.: 156ff.), in that 'perfect' rationality could only be attained progressively and slowly. Characteristic of the Age of Reason, he saw this process along the lines of 'voluntary' and 'involuntary' actions (ibid.: 116ff.); in the sense that every action of a totally rational person would be directed solely by voluntary thoughts (leading to voluntary actions), and that all individuals should endeavour to minimise and eventually eradicate involuntary actions. The only ancillary he deemed essential to this end was 'sincerity' (ibid.: 311ff.) betwixt people. Simply put, Godwin highlighted, for human rationality to work, individuals had to communicate their thoughts and problems with one another authentically and freely. Without this condition, 'Truth' would not be uncovered. It was for these reasons, as such, that Godwin's vision of the ideal did not find a higher authority necessary in itself.

Having said that, it must be equally noted what troubled Godwin was that authority on its own perpetuated a vicious cycle precluding reason from progress. By keeping individuals dependent on a body supposedly responsible for safeguarding freedom, governments themselves detract from that same freedom. According to Godwin, the main institutions contributing to this impediment comprised, amongst others, religious establishments (ibid.: 569ff.), law and punishment (ibid.: 642ff.), as well as property (ibid.: 701ff.); all working together towards the restraint of the individual. In this regard, Godwin thought, there was no difference between a government ruled by a monarch or one by elected representatives (ibid.: 248ff.). No matter what, each engendered similar symptoms: war and bloodshed, injustice and subjugation, a lack of virtue, so on and so forth. All complemented by the fact, these outcomes would remain permanently unchanged, due to the unlikelihood of escaping that vicious cycle which requires individuals to relinquish their freedom and independence as part of their 'social contract' with the state for the supposed, if not spurious, good of the community (ibid.: 212ff.).

At this point, it must be additionally noted that although Godwin advocated individual freedom as his primary value, he was equally aware of the positive significance — within social structures — of concepts such as morality, justice, and even equality among people as necessary values (ibid.: 165ff.). It goes without saying that in spite of the apparent conceptual contradistinction between the former and the latter from a libertarian's perspective, Godwin's compromise (even if not amply compelling) was that these latter values would eventually prove congenial, admittedly, once individuals began to understand their import by way of 'enlightened reason' (ibid.: 165). Obviously, in this regard, as Godwin thought his conclusions were gained rationally, he was not only certain of their 'Truth' but believed others also would soon come to realise them through the course of their own logic and intellect. In this vein, he presumed a knowledge once gained could never be discarded; a person who has, thus, grasped the logic of morality would never attempt to undertake antithetical actions thereafter (ibid.: 109).

Having recounted the fundamental points of *Political Justice*, it has to be said that, although Godwin may have been the first principal anarchist thinker, his particular views do not comprise the whole of anarchist thought by any means. Rather, as indicated more accurately by Suissa (2010: 11), anarchism should be viewed in terms of the 'individualist-socialist continuum'. Under this framework, it may be observed evidently, Godwin no doubt would fit near the individualist end of the spectrum as opposed to the communitarian end. An obvious difference, certainly, which is chiefly predicated on the varying degrees of priority given, on the one end, to the individual, or, on the other, to the social (ibid.: 25ff.). Hence, as connoted earlier, while Godwin clearly agreed on the importance of freedom as well as equality, justice, and duty to others, his starting point really was with individual freedom (personal autonomy and rationality) as opposed to the latter values (ibid.: 29).

By contrast, anarchist thinkers on the socialist end of the spectrum, comprising, for instance, Peter Kropotkin (1842–1921) and Mikhail Bakunin (1814–1876), believed the individualist assumption to be utterly ignorant of 'human society, the real starting point of all human civilisation and the only medium in which the personality and liberty of man can really be born and grow' (Bakunin cited in ibid.: 29). Kropotkin (1987), in this vein, especially suggested 'mutual aid', in defiance of 'competition', to be the defining characteristic of human history and a crucial part of its evolution and 'natural selection'. Put simply, he observed — from his surveys amid the 19th-century steppes and wildernesses of Russia and Siberia — survival and evolution amongst animals, birds, and insects depend not on their individual strength per se, but on their social ability to mutually support and aid one another (ibid.: 21ff.). This, admittedly, is the reason Kropotkin (in his final analysis) prioritised such values as equality, fraternity, solidarity, benevolence, and mutual aid among people above everything else (ibid.).

However, it is important to stress that even though the difference between individualist and socialist anarchists initially implies something of an anti-anarchist tension in terms of a hierarchy of values (Suissa, 2010: 50f.), the issue is resolved by the fact that within the anarchist ideal of decentralised (non-authoritative) networks, 'certain points and certain lines may be bolder than others, but none of them functions as a centre from which the others emerge or to which they return' (Todd May cited in ibid.: 51); suggesting, in consequence, the anarchist 'philosophical position that no one value, or goal, can be regarded as logically prior or ultimate' (ibid.).

So conjectured, before turning to an investigation of what education in anarchism entails, it merits to keep in mind, criticisms against authority equally extend beyond the confines of classical thinkers and classical arguments. In this respect, the late Ivan Illich's (1926–2002) 'accusatory' view on the capitalist institutions of modern Western culture and politics are probably worth mentioning here, as a brief illustration of a contemporary anarchist's objections contra 'structural' authority (as distinct from Illich's 'epistemic' and 'functional' understanding of authority endorsed by his 'learning networks'; different understandings of authority are discussed in greater detail in Part III).

In summation, Illich (1971: 1ff.) propounded that various sectors in society under the control of — a capitalist — government, from education and health care, all the way through to the police and the military, in all their entirety, had merely become consumer-oriented 'institutions'; a process that broadly focused on obligatory and 'ritualised' length of attendance, performance statistics, and certification, instead of any type of actual substance or quality; all leading, ineluctably, to a general degradation and misery in public life (ibid.: 1). He termed this overall process as 'schooling', broadly, in relation to every institutionalised faction of society and, specifically, in relation to education; underlying, thereby, the crucial task for an all-encompassing 'deschooling' (deinstitutionalisation) project to achieve some level of development towards that sense of (autonomous) self- and community-reliance necessary for people's 'liberation' (ibid.: 47). Along the lines of anarchist thought, he believed a process with this end in mind had to start, most probably, through education (as illustrated next).

Part II: Anarchist Education

Education plays a pivotal role in anarchism preponderantly because of the latter's conception of human nature, which is that humans are born neither good nor bad, and that they have the potential to become both — albeit never on a permanent basis — depending on circumstances (Suissa, 2010: 24ff.). In this spirit, as Kropotkin (1987: 24) pertinently stated: 'Rousseau had committed the error of excluding the beak-and-claw fight from his thoughts; and [Thomas] Huxley committed the opposite error; but neither Rousseau's optimism nor Huxley's pessimism can be accepted as an impartial interpretation of nature', according to which '[s]ociability [or virtue] is as much a law of nature as mutual struggle [or vice]'.

Godwin (1985: 96), by the same token, stated that 'the characters of men [sic.] originate in their external circumstances'. In this manner, very much characteristic of his abstract thinking, not only did he negate innate principles as 'superfluous', 'unsatisfactory' and 'absurd', but also instincts, alongside 'effects of antenatal impressions and original structure', as completely erroneous (ibid.: 96ff.). Besides, as he put singular stress on individual rationality, 'rational' education for Godwin played a fundamental role as a contributing 'circumstance' towards achieving and maintaining his ideal society. Broadly speaking, one anticipates education for anarchism is a means by which people's good nature is brought to the fore, and their unpalatable thoughts (or attitudes) are minimised at the same time (akin to Godwin's belief in voluntary and involuntary actions, as alluded to previously).

Nevertheless, education, as it is customarily delivered by the state, is not deemed 'acceptable' in anarchist eyes. Godwin, in particular, had in mind three criticisms defying national education. Firstly, that '[t]hey *actively* [italics added] restrain the flights of mind, and fix it in the belief of exploded errors' by producing permanence of opinion, *ergo* preventing rational thought (ibid.: 614). Secondly, that there is an inconsistency between the 'nature of mind' and nature of national education, in that knowledge learned independently and autonomously (in keeping with individualist anarchist thought) is likely to be more effective than knowledge gained by the instructions of another person (ibid.: 616). And, thirdly, Godwin questioned if preceptors within national education could truly teach anti-hierarchical values when they themselves worked within an environment essentially framed by the hierarchies of the state (ibid.: 617). Along the same lines, one might then ask, how can people of this sort 'sincerely' infuse students with values that lie outside the dominant political and social framework within which they instruct? In a phrase, that is to say, Godwin thought national education was simply 'the mirror and tool of national government' (ibid.: 612).

Naturally, this leads to an important question regarding the precise form an anarchist education should be expected to take in principle and in practice. Yet, what one may not initially realise is that there is neither a satisfactorily explicit strategic answer nor a satisfactorily explicit tactical answer to this question (at least on a first glimpse). In fact, according to Suissa (2010: 77), there is no single blueprint that could precisely be used to characterise the ideal anarchist education, either for individualist anarchists or socialist anarchists.

In this connexion, commencing with individualist anarchists like Godwin (1985: 111), while they appreciate the influence of education on balance, they ultimately seem to hold evident obscurities about its form and shape, if not its definition. After all, Godwin did not simply narrow education to what he termed 'national education'. He perceived it, rather broadly, both in the sense of 'the education of accident', in other words, the impressions one inescapably receives from the environment, independently of the preceptor; as well as in terms of nutrition and personal care children needfully receive from parents during their dependent years (ibid.: 765). For his part, Godwin's preferred alternative, in some measure likening to a touch of anarchist 'elitism' (Kramnick, 1985: 54), was Truth made available by 'the enlightened segment of society [...] to the great majority who are still under the spell of society's authoritarian institutions'; while, as an extreme gradualist, he rejected 'the use of force as an effective tool for social progress' (Clarke, 1975: 162). As evidence of his 'elitism', Godwin warned 'of the danger of large assemblies in which "persons of eminence, distinction, and importance [i.e. intelligentsia]" are not present' (ibid.: 163). At any rate, it is interesting to observe Godwin probably saw himself in this light, especially in view of his regular engagements with the political literati at the time focusing on such matters as the French Revolution and its potential counterpart in the British Isles (Kramnick, 1985: 10ff.). So said, as far as Godwin's individualist outlook and opposition to external intervention are concerned, only individuals themselves are thought best fit to undertake their own learning, at the same time as benefiting from the knowledge of the 'enlightened'.

With that in mind, it is important to note, as Godwin's perspective would probably not appease anarchist activists — say, in line with Malatesta — seeking immediate change in society, it is additionally useful to look into specific strategies from other (non-violent) sources similar to the same tradition. The suggestions of Ivan Illich, incidentally, are a good illustration in this particular case. Principally, to begin with, Illich (1971: vii) recommended the idea of educational 'webs' (rather than educational 'funnels' through specified instructions) built across the globe, and premised around four distinct attributes. The first of these, summarily, was an assortment of educational resources (ranging from books and libraries to computers) made available to the general public (ibid.: 79ff.). The second was creating contacts between students and experts to provide the former with opportunities to observe specialised skills by adept professionals; on its merits, Illich thought this process would allow students to learn more effectively than if they observed an unseasoned teacher (ibid.: 87). The third attribute, in turn, concerned developing networks between potential peers engrossed in similar topics to improve understanding through collaborative interaction and exploration in a progressive manner (ibid.: 91ff.); while the final attribute related to a 'master-student' association in which knowledge would be transmitted from the experienced mentor to the less experienced disciple — albeit in an epistemic and functional fashion, as noted earlier (ibid.: 97ff.). Illich's ideal, consequently, in compliance with Godwin's individualist philosophy, entailed a combination of the aforesaid attributes, ensuring a learning environment free from the limitations of an 'institutionalised' school and 'instructive' teaching, but aiming at informative interactions towards the successive build-up of knowledge in the offing.

Aside from the individualist anarchists, it is vital not to forget the other end of the spectrum, *vis-à-vis* social anarchists who underscore the importance of social education for achieving as well as maintaining the anarchist ideal. Encouragingly, on this matter, it is noteworthy numberless anarchist schools have undeniably existed in the past: a few cases in point being the *Escuela Moderna* in Barcelona (1901–1906) founded by Francisco Ferrer; the Modern School in New York and Stelton; not to mention the schools founded by Paul Robin, Sebastien Faure, and Madeline Vernet in France (Suissa, 2010: 93). Although there are several accounts of these schools in various sources (see ibid. for references), the famous Summerhill School (founded by A. S. Neill in 1921 in Suffolk), as 'the longest-lived libertarian educational project' (ibid.), is a good example to explore as a *starting point* on the path to a punctilious understanding of what an anarchist school may look like in practice — even though Summerhill does not describe itself as an anarchist school.

To start with, the most obvious hallmark of Summerhill School is there are no school curriculums whatsoever. Children are not, in this fashion, required to attend any lessons at any time during their stay at the School. As long as children's actions do not harm or interfere with the actions of others, they are free to do as they wish. They can play games, music or sport, dance, act, work, or do nothing at all (Neill, 1969: 3ff.). Either way, they are neither punished nor rewarded (ibid.: 162ff.). Teachers, cordially, are supposed to treat children with love, respect, honesty, and, above all, equality. Moreover, pursuant to Reichian psychoanalytic therapy, Neill assumed innumerable emotional, psychological, and psychosomatic issues such as crime, hate, jealousy, unhappiness, lying, etcetera, etcetera (see ibid.: 95ff.), to arise from a lack of knowledge into sexuality, as well as the repression of corresponding emotions — in the unconscious — in response to societal taboos (ibid.: 207). Accordingly, he believed, by fulfilling children's ego — and thereby happiness — within a safe and free environment, Summerhill School gave its children the requisite emotional wherewithal to pursue their real interests, no matter what, henceforth.

With those factors being noted, however, Summerhill School is not an anarchist school at the end of the day, and the main reason for this is that within anarchist education, there is an expectation to explore overarching anarchist values spoken of earlier, like freedom, equality, and fraternity (Suissa, 2010: 93ff.). Summerhill School, conversely, lacks a serious discussion on political matters, which ultimately is contrary to anarchism's underlying conception of freedom, construed in terms as carrying 'concrete political connotations' (Smith in ibid.: 94). Therefore, strictly speaking, anarchist education is not a politically-neutral position, under any circumstance, neither amidst individualist anarchists nor social anarchists. Its aim, rather, (as a politics-laden education) is progress towards the anarchist ideal, and its maintenance when that ideal is eventually achieved.

Part III: Counterarguments

To reiterate an erstwhile reflection, the individualist-socialist spectrum doubtlessly holds innumerable variations, across the length of its course, in the means and ends of education. Obviously, some of these have already been investigated in the previous section. Yet, with this background, there still is a need to further scrutinise some of that continuum's more questionable aspects if we are to acquire a fully-balanced account of things. In which occurrence, it is important to recognise, both ends of the anarchist spectrum share areas of 'overlapping' shortcomings. Before we probe into any aspect of suchlike convergences, however, a notable remonstration (specially maintained by libertarians) pertaining, specifically, to social anarchists' perception and application of education should be noted.

Namely, this concerns the idea that education as an inevitable wellspring of authority avowedly contradicts, from the very outset, anarchism's general hostility to oppressive hierarchies, and thereupon authority itself (ibid.: 57f.). Briefly, this stems from the notion that teaching such moral and political values as equality, mutual aid, and fraternity, technically speaking, infringes upon an individual's autonomy to think freely and independently; all through a system distinguished by a 'monopoly' on knowledge, which, in the strictest sense, would be considered anti-anarchist in nature.

In response, however, one may readily contend from a conceptual perspective, due to the 'decentralised' nature of anarchism, social anarchist education, properly speaking, operates from bottom to top, as opposed to the other way around. Accordingly, should leadership or authority ever be required for any development or function, necessities would be assessed on each occasion as and when needed, and attained organically, though never on a permanent basis. Conveniently, Suissa (2010: 58) has depicted this approach in the form of 'concentric circles', divided into two parts: whereupon the 'inner circle' would comprise 'the self-governing, face-to-face community, where social arrangements [are] established to meet the needs of this community'; while the 'outer circle' would typify 'federated coordination' with other communities, purely to fulfil the needs of those in the 'inner circle'. In this context, Suissa notes, authority may immediately be 'dismantled or rearranged' if it fails to realise its purposes (ibid.). This, in brief, is the crucial conceptual argument in defence of (social) anarchism's interpretation of authority applied to educational praxis.

That issue being addressed, however, another clear censure against the anarchist idea is its supposed utopian nature. Specifically, there is a prevalent belief that the goals set towards an education based on anarchist principles by ways of either the 'individualist' or 'socialist' methods are difficult, if not impossible, to achieve due to their alleged impracticality, as well as lack of a clear blueprint — as discussed before. What is more, one may call to attention the fact few anarchist schools or educational systems have successfully survived, heretofore, to lend any serious credibility to the anarchist conception of education.

Suissa, nevertheless, argues the charges of utopianism raised against anarchism assume there is veritably an element of the former at its core (ibid.: 139ff.). Rather, utopianism is a position that seeks as the end-goal a precise image of the ideal (Berlin in ibid.: 141). In this sense, utopian schemes of perception do not apply to anarchism, because the anarchist ideal is not based around a coherent picture of the perfect. This is for the simple reason, anarchism's conception of human nature, *in toto*, is perpetually variable (ibid.). What sets anarchism apart from a particularly narrow notion of utopianism (as drawn from Berlin, for example), essentially, is its express emphasis on experimentation and constant progress in development and improvement according to situational circumstances (ibid.). It is this quality that reconciles the supposed tension between anarchism's lack of a blueprint and utopian thought thereat.

That said, while anarchism's quandary with utopianism may appear resolved on a conceptual level, there naturally remains considerable doubt about its chances of success in practice. One of the best accounts of how things may go wrong with freedom-inspired movements is Edmund Burke's (2009: 76ff.) *Reflections on the Revolution in France*. For starters, Burke regarded 'Tradition' above all other things. In this vein, he deemed liberty (even if not in the sense proposed by anarchists) gave individuals too little control over their passions or natural instincts, and that it impaired virtue, dignity, and other noble values and principles preserved by tradition in society (ibid.: 76ff.). The French Revolution, in his opinion (and rightly, if one may dare say so), was a pertinent illustration of the things that could occur with the levelling of ancient, but time-tested edifice of traditional values.[1] Here, Burke argues, individuals in seeking liberty and autonomy broke away from that 'long line of wisdom' provided by their forbearers, with the fatal sequent that they were led to a volatile society incarnated by self-interested, egoistic bodies committing violence and murder by the sway of their temporary passions or emotions (Mitchell, 2009: xv). It was for this reason, Burke (2009: 91ff.) testified to the significance of preserving such traditional establishments as the Church, state, monarchy, and aristocracy to safeguard harmony and stability among the populace. Apropos to this, if the different strata in society (to wit, both higher and lower ranks) performed the functions given to them by tradition, values like justice, dignity, wisdom, and liberty would follow spontaneously (ibid.: 76ff.). The clear implication for anarchism being, accordingly, not just that individual autonomy must, hopelessly, remain inferior to traditional values, but that education should, itself, seek to reinforce those traditions.

---

[1] Criticisms of contemporary social movements adopting anarchist goals and methods are relevant here as well. For example, regarding the Occupy movement (another being the Arab Spring), conservatives viewed 'the Wall Street protesters as envious ingrates looking for government handouts because they fear responsibility' (Hartman, 2011).

Clearly, thence, Burke held human nature under the pessimistic sensibility that humans cannot, frankly, be trusted to manage their own affairs according to their own prudence. In some ways, whilst this judgment is probably far too harsh on human nature, there is insufficient evidence to back the contrary.[2] Even among anarchists themselves, there is clear uncertainty about the timescale in which things can sincerely be realised. Godwin (1985: 289ff.), in fact, believed true advance towards anarchism would be a slow and gradual process. In this regard, unlike anarchists favouring riotous methods for quick results, he actively opposed any type of violence or revolution, despite knowing his ideal might take hundreds of years to materialise by consequence (ibid.: 266). As a matter of principle, rather, he believed only through rational thinking could sensible steps be gradually taken towards a peaceful, stateless society. By the same token, no doubt, some social anarchists, like Kropotkin, whilst stressing human nature's dual standard, have showcased an equal awareness of the said problems in Burke's account. As Kropotkin (1987: 82) stated, for instance, '[u]nbridled individualism is a modern growth', even if it is not a primitive human characteristic. It should not be forgotten either, that the political climate in the West today has been dominated by liberalism and the liberal state in recent history (Suissa, 2010: 134ff.). Against this background, observably, one wonders if anarchist societies are a genuine possibility in our time. In any event, what is important to note is that accurate analyses of anarchism's future require that the (oft-neglected) slowness in human progress is taken into account at all times, particularly in view of Burke's criticism of freedom and defence of tradition.

Having said that, before terminating this section, it is worth noting a potential defence for anarchism in this connection. As

---

[2] Admittedly, as success stories, genuine popular uprisings in human history, such as Russia in 1917 and Hungary in 1956, were all characterised by autonomous direct action, decentralised decision-making, and free federation, which were then destroyed by the very party that rode them to power on fundamentally anarchist slogans, like 'All Power to the Soviets' (Ward, 1996: 28).

Justin Mueller (2012: 24) points out, 'anarchist schools have had an oft-troubled history of opposition and harassment from the powers-that-be': a good example being, of course, the *Escuela Moderna*, which was not only shut down by the Spanish authorities (in 1906), its founder, Ferrer, was also falsely accused of insurrection in Barcelona and executed in 1909 (Suissa, 2010: 81f.). Although it is evident anarchists pose an open threat to states' continued existence, if their activities did not work, for all intents and purposes, there would be little reason for authorities to attack them in the first place. One is, therefore, led to believe the 'powers-that-be' are presumably careful about the general influence of anarchism because it really does pose a danger; indicating, on this ground, the ideal anarchist education (individualist and especially social) may not be so separate from the facts of reality, after all. So expressed, one alarmingly wonders what might possibly occur to Summerhill School if it ever began curricula promoting anarchist values!

Conclusion

All things considered, anarchism is undoubtedly a fascinating, if not an enticing, political position in and of itself. Yet, notwithstanding this attraction, under the present political and cultural circumstances, many are also inclined to consider it utopian. It is this factor, ultimately, that undermines (if not prevents) anarchism's ability to achieve its goals today. Nevertheless, it is worth bearing in mind (against this framework) even though we may not be able to effectuate an anarchist society now, it does not mean we should be discouraged from applying anarchist-inspired 'micro-level strategies' and perhaps non-violent direct action locally, within and without schools. After all, this would not only be in line with Illich's hypothesis that change in society should first arise from education, but also Abraham DeLeon's (2008: 124ff.) suggestion that small-scale direct action can eventually ensure a gradual, though advancing materialisation towards a tangible anarchist society.

To briefly recapitulate, this essay has contributed to the literature on anarchist education in a three-fold manner. Firstly, while Godwin no doubt is mentioned in this literature, he ordinarily seems to be overshadowed by social anarchists. Certainly, although there are good reasons for this (for instance, social anarchism's larger focus on education), it should not be forgotten that Godwin's ideas and thoughts run through the whole of the anarchist movement, as shown during the span of this essay. It is suggested, therefore, to revisit Godwin more often in the interest of potential researches on anarchist education in the future. Secondly, the same may be said about the work of Burke, whose pessimistic, if not realistic, understanding of human nature poses a considerable challenge to anarchism's journey before it even begins. Burke's observations, essentially, provide a somewhat fresh criticism against anarchist education, which must not be neglected. Finally, as perhaps the most significant contribution, the fact that anarchist attempts at education, overall, have been transparently attacked by those in power — thusly preventing anarchism's progress in its tracks — showcases an important part of the history of anarchism: that, perhaps, it is not as utopian as we might suppose an anarchist society to be even under present circumstances. The literature, whence, might benefit from a review of historical facts to support future outcomes. To conclude, therewith, a large task undeniably lies ahead in demonstrating the full potential of anarchism. Through its contribution to the literature on anarchist education via the three foregoing ways, this paper has hopefully succeeded in part towards this long-term process.

BIBLIOGRAPHY

Burke, E. 2009. *Reflections on the Revolution in France*. Oxford: Oxford University Press.

Clarke, J. P. 1975. 'On Anarchism in an Unreal World: Kramnick's View of Godwin and the Anarchists'. *The American Political Science Review* 69 (1), pp. 162-167.

DeLeon, A. 2008. 'Oh No, Not the 'A' word! Proposing an 'Anarchism' for Education'. *Educational Studies* 44 (2), pp. 122-141.

Godwin, W. 1985. *Enquiry Concerning Political Justice: And Its Influence on Modern Morals and Happiness* (3rd edition). Middlesex: Penguin Books.

Hartman, A. 2011. 'Occupy Wall Street: A New Culture War?'. *The Chronicle of Higher Education*, 12 November. Available at: https://www.chronicle.com/article/Occupy-Wall-Street-A-New/129695/, (Accessed 1 February 2019).

Illich, I. D. 1971. *Deschooling Society*. London: Calder & Boyars. pp. 7-54.

Kramnick, I. 1985. Introduction. In: William Godwin, (3rd edition) *Enquiry Concerning Political Justice: And Its Influence on Modern Morals and Happiness*. Middlesex: Penguin Books, pp. 7-54.

Kropotkin, P. 1987. *Mutual Aid: A Factor of Evolution*. London: Freedom Press.

Malatesta, E. 1894. 'Anarchy and Violence'. *The Anarchist Library*. Available at: https://theanarchistlibrary.org/library/errico-malatesta-anarchy-and-violence (Accessed 1 January 2019).

McLaughlin, P. 2007. *Anarchism and Authority: A Philosophical Introduction to Classical Anarchism*. Aldershot: Ashgate Publishing.

Mitchell, L. G. 2009. Introduction. In: Edmund Burke, *Reflections on the Revolution in France*. Oxford: Oxford University Press, pp. vii-xix.

Mueller, J. 2012. Anarchist, the State, and the Role of Education. In Robert H. Haworth, (ed.) *Anarchist Pedagogies: Collective Actions, Theories, and Critical Reflections on Education*. Oakland CA: PM Press, pp. 14-31.

Neill, A. S. 1969. *Summerhill: A Radical Approach to Education*. London: Victor Gollancz.

Suissa, J. 2010. *Anarchism and Education: A Philosophical Perspective*. Oakland CA: PM Press.

Ward, C. 1996. *Anarchy in Action*. London: Freedom Press.

II. ON LANGUAGE AND THE 'EXTENDED-MIND' THEORY

> Being personally acquainted with a number of Waldorf students, I can say that they come closer to realizing their own potential than practically anyone I know.
> — *Professor Joseph Weizenbaum, a Father of Modern Artificial Intelligence*

It would be a mistake to deny that communication (of any description) lies at the centre of all human interactions. In this regard, words, of course, represent only one form of that interplay: tone of voice, facial expression, bodily movement, even silence, in a sense constitute disparate ways of communication — each, one might add, with changing degrees of relevance against different backdrops. Interestingly, that noticed, serious debates on language were discussed as early as authors dating back to Ancient Greece (for example, in Plato's texts) and before; although the subject has obviously gained increasing attention since, and particularly an upsurge at that in recent years amongst academics in fields ranging from philosophy and psychology to linguistics.

Amidst the latter group, to be sure, one that probably stands out is Andy Clark, author of the 'extended-mind' theory. This is a conception meant to diminish the mind-world division typically associated with Descartes. In rudimentary terms, Clark's assertion is that the mind 'extends' beyond the skull — and into the world

— due to the unique function of 'external tools' that augment cognitive performance. In this regard, having caused no small controversy in academia, the theory especially appraises language as perhaps the most important 'tool' in this process, in a fashion that if one must consider the best way to unravel any controversies, one is unavoidably bound to investigate Clark's viewpoint of language, above all, as the central point-of-reference.

With that circumstance in mind, the aim of this chapter is to assess the role of language with reference to the work of Andy Clark on the extended-mind, as well as a wider range of other sources concerning, almost, the entire spectrum of thought on the matter. To be more precise, it is divided into three sections. The first part sets out Clark's overall notion of the extended-mind and its implications on the functions of language. The second, thereafter, examines criticisms of the extended-mind and extrapolates the 'communicative conception' of language, while the final part draws from Wittgenstein's later work on language for a more radical assessment as such. It is concluded that Wittgenstein offers a better, more accurate alternative to both the 'communicative conception' of language and the extended-mind theory of Clark and that future studies on language should try to revisit Wittgenstein more often.

Part I: The 'Extended-Mind' and Language

To gain a better picture of Clark's analysis of language, it is useful, at the outset, to delineate the concept of the extended-mind. To that end, we shall begin by observing that the root of this concept, actually, lies in the work of several figures, including Martin Heidegger, Maurice Merleau-Ponty, Lev Vygotsky, not to mention Laura Berk, Peter Carruthers, and Daniel Dennett, all of whom have appeared to advocate, in some way or other, the so-called 'supra-communicative' view of language (Clark, 1997: xvii; 1998: 163); the basic principle being, briefly, that while communication makes up some portion of what is considered to be the role of language, there is far more to it than might be seen at first glance (Clark, 1998: 163ff.).

As it happens, moreover, the diminishing influence of so-called Cartesian dualism — as an additional background against Clark's theory of the extended-mind — has been due in part to the emergence of recent 'coalition of sciences of the mind' that are collectively known as cognitive sciences (Clark, 1997: xi). Each of these suppose that the 'mind arises out of the workings of a physical machine' (ibid.). Indeed, drawing on the research around artificial intelligence, Clark argues the reason 'the best of our "intelligence" artefacts [… are] unspeakably, terminally dumb' is because the mind has been primarily imagined as a 'logical reasoning device' comprised of data, rather than 'an organ for controlling the biological body' (ibid.: 1). It is for this reason, by the way, that Clark is critical of such multi-million projects like CYC ('encyclopedia') that have focused on quantity in knowledge, rather than — quality in — any 'basic kinds of adaptive responses to [or coupling with] an environment' (ibid.: 3).

Essentially, the new model proposes that the environment itself is important in terms of guiding the creature, in cooperation with onboard circuitry and simple adaptive intelligence (ibid.: 14f.). Put differently, Clark suggests, 'mini-brains' would need to link together in order to ensure a 'globally coherent behaviour', independently of such characteristics as a central executive control (or serial planning), leading in consequence to spontaneity and fast, real-time response (ibid.: 17, 21). By extension, also, the information-processing load is reduced through the gradual 'sensitising' of the system to specific environmental features (ibid.: 24). Needless to say, when applied to human beings,[3] Clark continues that while 'much of human intelligence is based on similar environment-specific tricks and strategies' as well as action, we have the additional advantage of 'linguistic, logical and geometric formalisms' (ibid.: 31, 62). Parenthetically, the body is perceived 'as part of the computational loop' (ibid.: 84).

---

[3] Somewhat like 'natural-born cyborgs' (Clark, 2001: 24).

It is along the lines of this framework that the extended-mind has really taken shape as a concept. In order to appreciate Clark's argument about language augmenting cognition, it is first necessary to understand his concept of the extended-mind. As briefly mentioned before, the idea is that any external prop outside the brain, like notes in a personal diary or smartphone, road signs, books, and reminders, which help reduce cognitive load, fundamentally augment (or complement) the performance of the brain. The Inga-Otto thought experiment, to exemplify Clark's extended-mind theory, demonstrates how one's diary can play an identical role to memory, say, in reminding oneself of a location's address (Adams and Aizawa, 2010: 3). Likewise, to add another illustration, the process involved in writing books involves many external props, such as files, papers, notes, and so on, to fully actuate the finalised text (Clark, 1997: 207). Clark, therefore, in simple terms, views the extended-mind in relation to problem-solving involving processes of reasoning and acting across the mind-world boundary (ibid.: 68). Integral to all of this is the use of language but not simply for purposes of communication.

Crucially then, Clark stands opposed to the apparent Cartesian dualism between the mind on one side, and the world on the other (ibid.: xi). The hypothesis wants to breach that traditional division by 'extending' the mind through the skull and flesh into the world. In which case, Clark contends, the local environment, including our physical bodies, effectively become 'extensions' of the mind as they actively build 'into the processing loops that result in intelligent action' (ibid.: xii). Clark, so to speak, sees the mind as a leaky, permeable organ (ibid.: 53).

Those concepts being stated, it is time now to turn to Clark's understanding of language according to his theory of the extended-mind. Overall, whilst language gets a minimal treatment as any other external tool that helps improve cognitive performance, Clark is nevertheless quick to characterise language as 'the ultimate artefact' by means of which one alters the 'nature of the computational tasks' in problem-solving, without transfiguring the brain's fundamental features, namely modes of representation and 'experiential' space (ibid.: 193; Clark, 1998: 180). In a sense, by reshaping a broad range of difficult and complex tasks into formats suitable for the fundamental 'computational capacities of the human brain', namely 'pattern recognition and transformation', language enables us to reach higher intellectual and behavioural horizons (Clark, 1997: 194).

Either way, to be more specific, Clark (1998: 166) argues 'linguistic artefacts' magnify the activities of our 'pattern-completing brains' in six major ways. One way relates to the so-called 'path dependency', which supposes that learning is dependent on early cases of training (Clark, 1997: 204). In this respect, Clark stresses, the communicative role of language allows human cognition to become collective, enabling 'culturally scaffolded reason […] to incrementally explore spaces' inaccessible to path-dependent individual reason (ibid.: 206). Second, Clark states language can augment the use of the brain's basic cognitive resources through inner speech, particularly in terms of attention and resources allocation, as an extra 'control loop' (ibid.: 202). One example, in this connection, is 'high-level concerns or policies' (maxims) that are usually used by Tetris (a digital game) experts in an effort to enhance their performance in the game by assisting them in their ability to 'focus, monitor and control behaviour (ibid.: 203; Clark, 1998: 173). Subsequently, another way is about 'data manipulation and representation' (Clark, 1998: 173). To illustrate this point, Clark uses the example of writing actual texts (chapter in a book), arguing that 'printed words and symbols allows us to search, store, sequence and re-organise data' in a manner separate from the normal workings of the biological brain (ibid.).

Fourth, the above noted, perhaps the most obvious of the six ways, on the whole, is in regards to 'memory augmentation', which refers to the use of texts, notebooks, diaries, and so on in order to store some large and complex data for the purpose of recall at some point in the future (Clark, 1998: 169). The fifth way, with that stated, is about 'environmental simplification' (ibid.: 170). Clark notes that there are two aspects to this point: one is in relation to 'the use of labels' as simple clues to help 'negotiate complex environments', for example, signs for city centres, nightclubs, and cloakrooms; whereas the other relates to the provision of a 'simplified *learning environment*' (emphasis in original), vis-à-vis the application of linguistic labels, in order to speed (or enable) understanding in things that might lie outside our (immediate) intellectual horizons, such as a black hole, charity, or extortion (ibid.). The sixth, finally, is regarding 'co-ordination and the reduction of on-line deliberation' (ibid.: 171). This involves not only linguistic exchange to plan and co-ordinate activities, both at intra- as well as inter-personal levels, but to effectively decrease one's 'daily on-line deliberation' through explicit plans that reduce the cognitive load needed to go about one's daily business (ibid.).

All in all, additionally, the six ways revolve around two broad themes: one is the use of language (in text or speech) as forms of external workspace or memory; the other is the role of language in transforming the shape of the computational and cognitive spaces wherein we inhabit (ibid.: 174). As Clark himself admits, the second theme is the more neglected of the two, while the first is self-explanatory (ibid.). Hence, to expand the latter, it is significant Clark associates words with 'filters' in that through an association of a simple word (an external item) with an idea, complex knowledge is effectively frozen into something of a 'cognitive building block', which can then be used as a primary base-line for thought, search and learning in the future (ibid.). In other words, Clark supposes, like a 'perceptual modality', simple tags and labels actually render 'our world concrete and salient', thereby allowing us to focus thoughts along with 'learning algorithms' on basic objects gained under a new domain (ibid.: 175).

Lastly, it is worth noting, Clark (1997: 208) takes this idea even further by stating that words, not unlike an island grown from a mangrove seed (as opposed to the inverse process of an island providing what is necessary for the seed to grow), can sometimes determine thoughts, when expressed in a poem. Such a supra-communicative account of language, therefore, rejects the view that language expresses ideas that are already understood and formulated in the brain (Clark, 1998: 165). In which case, Clark conjectures that perhaps it is public language that leads to 'second-order cognitive dynamics', involving such things as self-criticism and self-evaluation (Clark, 1997: 208). This 'thinking about thinking', Clark suggests, is a consequence of thought becoming an object in itself through the use of words, exposing it to further mental operations, whereby different elements are picked out and scrutinised individually, enabling us to advance cognitive achievements (ibid.: 209f.). All of this is made possible by the development of a code that is suitably memorable, context-resistant, and modality-transcending, allowing for the scrutiny of an object from a range of distinct cognitive angles (Clark, 1998: 178). Obviously, this contrasts with the initial question about language as a means for communication only, in view of the multi-faceted way described in this section.

In a few words then, for Clark, language as perhaps the most significant external tool (both in spoken or written format), and as something that extends the mind across the mind-world boundary, does not only facilitate communication between human beings, it inflates the cognitive performance of the brain and (sometimes), accordingly, shapes and determines our thoughts. Having said that, although the extended-mind may be an attractive concept at first sight, it has faced a number of criticisms nevertheless. The following section outlines the attacks of two authors, Frederick Adams and Kenneth Aizawa, on the concept of the extended-mind — which they term the extended-*cognition* — and uses that as a springboard to delve into the specific understandings of language from the point of view of the 'communicative conception'.

Part II: *The Communicative Conception of Language*

Adams and Aizawa have criticised the extended-mind theory specifically from the standpoint of cognitive psychology. Their argument, in short, while admitting it is not a 'full-blown' theory, is based around two hypotheses: that cognitive processes are specific, and that these operate on 'non-derived mental representations' (Adams and Aizawa, 2010: viii, ix). To begin with, regarding the first hypothesis, they suggest there is a difference in the underlying mechanisms between cognitive and non-cognitive processes, and that the former are typically brain-bound (intracranial), rather than spread over the boundaries of the body and environment (ibid.: 9f.). After all, neurons are not all the same in our entire physical body: nerves in the retina or the spinal cord are, needless to say, dissimilar to those in muscles (ibid.: 18f.). The second hypothesis, on the other hand, refers to the proposition that 'cognitive processes involve representations, which means what they do is in virtue of naturalistic conditions that do not include the content-bearing states, properties, or processes of other entities', as detailed further below (ibid.: 9). The authors maintain, in turn, that non-derived representations are found inside the brain and that, therefore, cognition is intracranial (ibid.: 9).

Relevantly, that said, Adams and Aizawa further criticise the extended-cognition (mind) theory in terms of inadequate attention to three distinctions. Firstly, they argue little differentiation is made between a causal connection and an actual process constituting part of the cognitive process (ibid.: 10). Simply put, just because a 'process Y' interacts with a cognitive process it does not infer that the former constitutes a part of the latter. Indeed, they call this misapprehension 'the coupling-constitution fallacy' (ibid.: ix, 11). Secondly, the authors point to the blurred distinction between the hypothesis of an extended 'cognitive system' and the hypothesis of an extended-cognition (ibid.: 11). Analogously, a machine will have different kinds of processes in different parts of its *system*. One cannot, therefore, simply go from one to the other without a clear delineation between system and process. The third inadequacy that the authors identify, to be certain, relates to the lack of plausible development concerning a theory of the cognitive and non-cognitive, which would do 'justice to the subject matter of cognitive psychology' (ibid.). An issue, to some extent, made worse by the lack of even a workable strategy toward achieving one (ibid.).

By extension, other than the above-named problems, the authors have equally questioned the contentions around 'complementarity' and 'evolution' that are sometimes used to advocate the extended-cognition (mind) hypothesis. The former asserts that because processes in the brain work well in combination with bodily and environmental processes — in fact, better than the brain on its own — then cognition extends into the body and environment (ibid.: 7f.). The latter, instead, states that if some of our cognitive features adapted to work in concord with the features of our environment through evolution, then those features should really constitute part of the mind's cognitive apparatus (ibid.: 8). Conversely, Adams and Aizawa argue neither of the two themes — complementarity or evolution — has any logical basis to assert that cognitive processes extend beyond the brain. This is because, first, 'the combination of cognitive processes in the brain with apparently non-cognitive processes found in tools' does not signify the whole process being regarded as entirely cognitive (ibid.: 12). And, second, evolution by natural selection cannot be expected to demonstrate anything about where cognitive processes might be found; that duty, instead, lies with a theory of cognition (ibid.).

Stated so, notwithstanding the foregoing critique of Adams and Aizawa, they do not, in fact, discuss language (its position, that is, in relation to the extended-cognition or mind) at any length. All they mention is that thoughts bear non-derived (or original) content and that natural language bears derived content (ibid.: 34). The distinction between derived and non-derived (original) content is that the former comes from intentional agents who already have thoughts with meaning, whereas the latter do not require the prior existence or independence of other intentional agents or representations (ibid.: 32). In this sense, because non-derived (original) mental representations are usually found inside the brain, cognition must typically be intracranial and vice versa. Put another way, the first mind (in a series that evolved) did not receive its thought content from other minds as there did not exist any for doing so at the beginning (Aizawa and Adams 2005: 662).

So, while gas gauges, traffic lights, and flags bear derived content outside the brain, experiences, thoughts, and perceptions bear non-derived content inside the brain (according to this theory). In terms of their theoretical framework, furthermore, although Adams and Aizawa both come from the angle of cognitive psychology, these points of reference essentially fit into the broader field of cognitive sciences, which are currently dominated by the literature on the communicative conception of language (Carruthers and Boucher, 1998: 1). It is with that in mind, by chance, that we shall now turn to a brief examination of one of two extreme ends of the continuum concerning the relationship between language and thought.

So, according to the communicative conception, language is primarily an adjunct to thought as well as belief (ibid.: 1). In this regard, perhaps the most notable proponent of the communicative conception of language is Noam Chomsky, whose influential work on linguistics has led him to think language possesses its own unique faculty in the brain. Particularly, that is, his approach appears to be that language is one among a variety of distinct components in a 'modular' structure, which specifically includes visual, auditory, touch, motor, and taste elements; alongside the so-called 'central' constituents comprising, namely, the 'theory of mind' (ibid.: 2). On the face of it, he indubitably affirms thought is both translated into language through linguistic expression, as well as translated out of language through linguistic comprehension into a 'language of thought' (ibid.: 9). In this fashion, grammar not only lies at the center of this process, but it is something that is inbuilt, rather than acquired or learned, which, of course, corresponds with the general idea of 'modules' in the brain.

The more traditional view of the communicative conception of language, expressly from a philosophical standpoint, can be witnessed in *Tractatus Logico-Philosophicus* (that is, *Treatise on Logic and Philosophy*) by Wittgenstein. The *Tractatus*, summarly, was concerned with the picture theory of meaning, while it declared: 'The primary function of language is to state what is the case', which 'makes up the world or reality' (Hamlyn, 1988: 305). Indeed, as put succinctly by Hamlyn, 'the case comprises, at bottom, a number of simple states of affairs, which are made up of simple objects; and these are represented by elementary propositions (ibid.)'. Thus, Wittgenstein (2010: 45ff.) essentially argued meaning is derived from pictures, and pictures, in turn, are made up of clear elementary facts, each corresponding to a word in a sentence. Thenceforth, Wittgenstein believed such things as aesthetics, ethics, love, and so forth, cannot ever be discussed since they are simply 'transcendental' (ibid.: 88). Under this earlier conception, thus, language serves only to facilitate the communication of 'pictures' between people, and nothing more (even though he radically changed his outlook when he later wrote *Philosophical Investigations*, as showcased in Part III).

Keeping the above account of the communicative conception of language at hand, one may also speak of an all-encompassing spectrum regarding the relation between language and thought (Carruthers and Boucher, 1998: 1ff.). Altogether, to be clear, on the one end of this spectrum, language is perceived *only* as a tool for communication, in line with the earlier interpretations of Chomsky and Wittgenstein; while the other end, manifestly, is dedicated to the so-called cognitive conception of language, which is the idea that language is the source of all thoughts. The region betwixt the two ends of this dichotomy, under that premise, consists of theories that are, predictably, weak forms of the two extremes. The extended-mind theory, to name a familiar example not falling on either end, is distinctly a weak form of the communicative conception of language, particularly in light of the supplementary role of language (according to Clark) in enhancing cognitive performance.

All the same, what is unequivocally interesting is that contemporary academic works on the aforesaid debate are increasingly becoming dominated by theories that fit into the midsection of the spectrum (ibid.: 11). In this vein, books like *Language and Thought* (ibid.), whilst offering a wide array of expert opinions that investigate the relationship between language and thought, are ultimately constrained in their lack of sufficient attention to extreme forms of the other end of the above-mentioned continuum, headed by the cognitive account. The section following, in consequence, strives to address this issue via an explication of Wittgenstein's later work, *Philosophical Investigations*, as one of the main driving forces behind the advent of the cognitive conception of language (even though that term itself might not, on second thought, sit well with Wittgenstein's theory).

Part III: Wittgenstein, Language, and Thought

Although the *Tractatus* and *Philosophical Investigations* are both about language, one is more likely to find the latter intriguing upon learning that Wittgenstein had radically revised his ideas in that work, after realising, as he plainly admitted there, he had made 'grave mistakes' in the former (Wittgenstein 2001: x^e). A curious development, without doubt, deserving further attention, especially when bearing in mind *Philosophical Investigations* is sometimes considered one of the most influential, if not revolutionary, works of philosophy in the 20th century, specifically about the significance of language (Richter, no date). With that mentioned, this section commences with a brief outline of Wittgenstein's later thoughts on language. Those ideas are then applied to criticise Clark, his critics, and the broader community of thinkers mentioned hitherto. Lastly, we examine potential critiques against *Philosophical Investigations* and provide possible responses.

To begin with, it is worth noting, Wittgenstein's goal with *Philosophical Investigations* was to take the debate on language significantly further than his earlier work, particularly in light of the emergence of his new conception about 'language-games'. Crucially, this time around, Wittgenstein (2001: 12^e) argued meaning was derived from the 'use', or 'application', of words rather than their picturing. In consequence, very much like tools in a toolbox, Wittgenstein believed a single word could be utilised in different contexts for different purposes, depending on the language-game within which words are being played. Accordingly, he noticed the call 'Slab!' might denote a range of different understandings on its own. So, for instance, the word might mean the object itself (slab), or alternatively an order to bring one, etcetera, etcetera (ibid.: 4ᵉ). In equal measure, to present something of a slightly unusual implication, one might insist that a Christian and an Atheist should not clash with one another simply because their language-games operate under different 'rules' (ibid.: 23ᵉ); rules (definitions and judgments) that are collectively accepted within their own specific community (Hamlyn, 1988: 312). All suggesting, eventually, that giving orders, reporting an event, guessing riddles, making up a story, and even tones of voice, facial expressions, and body movements may constitute language-games; each in their own special and unique way (Wittgenstein, 2001: 10ᵉ). For Wittgenstein, all intents and purposes considered, the entire process, including the interweaving of actions, naming, and repeating words, is a language-game overall (ibid.: 4ᵉ). The difference with the *Tractatus*, to compare the 'nitty-gritties', is that words are now positioned within a language-game, meaning they could not lose their essence, even in spite of hypothetical cases whereby the object itself ceased to exist under a particular set of circumstances (ibid.: 17ᵉ-18ᵉ).

Obviously, the theory of language being sketched has clear implications for Clark's extended-mind theory. A position imputing Clark's work is only a language-game, nothing else. Similarly, that noted, cognitive philosophy — as Clark's framework of reference — functions under two language-games: one based on rules in cognitive observation, the other inside philosophy; a combination of which is likely to result in confusion and misunderstanding. Either way, one might uphold, even the criticisms against the extended-mind theory are subconscious language-games *in toto*. When, therefore, Adams and Aizawa are criticising the extended-cognition (mind) theory, the authors do not seem to recognise that their critique is only a contrary language-game, notwithstanding any questions it may raise, say, with regards to the way cognitive and non-cognitive processes are defined, in their unique field of cognitive psychology — as yet another attempted combination of two language-games into one, cognitive science with psychology. What goes without saying is that almost any spectrum pointed out by any one of the afore-named authors — particularly Carruthers and Boucher regarding the relationship between language and thought — all in effect merely form a comparable language-game, and so on.

As a central figure in the historical development of analytic philosophy, Wittgenstein's primary aim throughout his life was to solve deep philosophical problems perennially haunting philosophers. Already, as mentioned in the previous section, he had tried this in the *Tractatus* by declaring 'transcendental' issues had to be discarded altogether as things without pictures. However, it was only with *Philosophical Investigations* when Wittgenstein, having altered his conceptual framework, proposed that the philosopher's object is to clarify thought by way of elucidating propositions within individual language-games (Hamlyn, 1988: 306). To Wittgenstein (2001: 16^e), in broad strokes, problems within philosophy arose when language 'goes on holiday'. It is against this context that while Clark and his opponents operate within the same Anglo-American analytic tradition, there appears to be an intentional conflict betwixt their language-games, when in fact there should not be any, according, that is, to Wittgenstein's overall assessment. Interestingly, Adams and Aizawa (2010: x) themselves seem to admit there is likely going to be an endless clash between their ideas and the proponents of the extended-mind. In all likelihood, without seeming to be aware of its background existence, they are acknowledging there is, as a matter of fact, a conflict between two language-games in play; one which they are sure 'will press on', and perhaps never lead to a resolution (ibid.: x).

By parallel measure, it is worth stressing, the same defence is equally applicable to such critiques of Wittgenstein involving case studies consisting of individuals affected by certain medical problems. One example, in this connection, is Varley's report regarding an 'a-grammatic aphasic' with poor grammatical structure processing who was able to pass tests for 'Theory of Mind' as well as 'causal reasoning', indicating — in a manner of speaking — that (propositional) thought might, despite Wittgenstein, be independent of language (Carruthers and Boucher, 1998c: 124). Another (albeit similar) example is delivered by Goldin-Meadow and Zheng, whose studies around deaf children using home-sign to express thoughts and emotions without any previous engagement with a conventional language model, seems to suggest that (at least some) thoughts can additionally be communicated irrespectively of language (Carruthers & Boucher, 1998b: 22f.).

Although these cases might initially look as though they weaken Wittgenstein's theory of language (by shifting the balance toward the communicative understanding of language), he personally would have counter-argued that all are language-games, while adding it would be impossible to express the chance of any separation of thought from language if language-games did not exist. Analogously, one may assert that what really goes on inside the minds of those (deaf or aphasic) individuals can only remain an epistemological mystery for us because there is no way to truly find out the content. Indeed, the problematic nature of any study regarding the relationship between language and thought is also made obvious through the work of recent scholars on language, particularly considering the collection of opposing results that different researchers have entailed so far. Even more notable is the fact that authors writing on this topic are somewhat unsure about their own findings, frequently stating that further research is required for 'firm conclusions' (Carruthers and Boucher, 1998a: 18).

All things considered, one cannot but be surprised that, no matter the rigour of his theory, Wittgenstein is mentioned only three times in passing throughout the entire edited book, *Language and Thought* (one of the more authoritative contemporary texts on the relation between language and thought), by Carruthers and Boucher, whose chapters are penned by 13 scholars from a diverse range of expertise. Whilst this is not to say that Carruthers and Boucher's collection of edited essays is pointless, it is crucial, surely, that authors in this broad field (cognitive science) focus on their own unique language-game, rather than clash with the language-games of others. The clear implication of this argument, following Wittgenstein's point of view, is that the two camps on the above-mentioned spectrum, and those remaining in the midsection, distance themselves from conflict and, instead, concentrate on a descriptive account of their own unique language-game. This should not only remove confusion in language, but ensure the right questions are being asked, as progress is made in research.

Conclusion

As alluded to earlier, there is little doubt the subject matter of language has been around for a long time. After all, while Saint Augustine commented on learning words, Plato — before him — was critical of the dilemmas of writing as an external 'tool'. Indeed, it is worth recalling that regardless of prioritising speech over writing altogether, because of what he saw as the 'authentic living presence of spoken language', Plato believed human beings were inescapably condemned to the mechanical and repetitive inscriptions of knowledge on an object (writing as opposed to verbal expression), essentially, as the only way to record, preserve and commemorate time-honoured lessons (to maintain them for future generations) (Norris, 1987: 30ff.). Incidentally, in a word, writing was referred to as *Pharmakon*, meaning 'cure' and 'poison' at the same time. At any rate, although Plato had different reasons to Clark, one is inclined to acquiesce that the extension of the mind beyond the brain is a necessity for us, no matter what, even if 'internal' knowledge might have been the preferred format in the eyes of some, like Plato and Socrates. Certainly, then, in spite of similarities in outcome between Plato's and Clark's (namely, the inevitability of, or need for, external 'tools' outside the brain), the latter is still important in our *current* paradigm of thought, which is characterised by an alliance between the traditional worlds of philosophy and psychology with the world of biology (Damasio, 1999: 12). Indeed, the federation of scientific approaches that has led to recent advances in understanding language, memory, and consciousness (ibid.), is comprised of works such as Clark's extended-mind theory.

To summarise, this paper has attempted to gauge the function of language from a threefold perspective. First, it detailed Adam Clark's extended-mind theory and its implications for language. Second, these were criticised by authors fitting into the general communicative understanding of language. Third, Wittgenstein's later thoughts were used to propose an alternative, more radical view, of the functions of language. On the whole, what happens to be the most recurrent theme in this paper is that language is *not* simply a means to communication. Contrariwise, language appears to play roles ranging from augmenting the cognitive performance of the brain, as proposed by Clark, to defining the entirety of human cognisance. Finally, come what may, the importance of Clark's contribution to recent literature on language, the significance of much-neglected arguments by Wittgenstein on language-games needs recalling; especially as Wittgenstein's momentous influence on 20th-century thought in Philosophy remains a challenge to current researchers, albeit a submerged provocation due to the fact that his ideas have lost influence in recent times. Nonetheless, one cannot simply ignore Wittgenstein's understanding of language. Simultaneously, one cannot disregard the evidence relating to his potent analysis of functional language from a paradigmatic point of view. In the words of Carruthers and Boucher (1998: 18), therefore, perhaps we are now at a stage 'to re-open old questions, and to raise new possibilities', but this time with regard to the telling implications of Wittgensteinianism on language.

BIBLIOGRAPHY

Adams, F., & Aizawa, K. 2010. *The Bounds of Cognition*. Chichester: Wiley-Blackwell.

Aizawa, K., & Adams, F. 2005. 'Defending Non-Derived Content'. *Philosophical Psychology* 18 (6), pp. 661-669.

Carruthers, P., & Boucher, J. 1998a. Introduction: opening up options. In: P. Carruthers & J. Boucher, eds. *Language and Thought: Interdisciplinary themes*. Cambridge: Cambridge University Press, pp. 1-18.

Carruthers, P., & Boucher, J. 1998b. Introduction to Part I. In: P. Carruthers & J. Boucher, eds. *Language and Thought: Interdisciplinary themes*. Cambridge: Cambridge University Press, pp. 21-25.

Carruthers, P., & Boucher, J. 1998c. Introduction to Part II. In: P. Carruthers & J. Boucher, eds. *Language and Thought: Interdisciplinary themes*. Cambridge: Cambridge University Press, pp. 123-127.

Clark, A. 1997. *Being There: Putting Brain, Body, and World Together Again*. Cambridge, Massachusetts: The MIT Press.

Clark, A. 1998. Magic words: how language augments human computation. In: P. Carruthers & Boucher, J., eds. *Language and Thought: Interdisciplinary themes*. Cambridge: Cambridge University Press, pp. 162-183.

Clark, A. 2001.' Reasons, Robots and the Extended Mind (Rationality for the New Millenium)'. *Mind and Language* 16 (2), pp. 121-145.

Damasio, A. 1999. *The Feeling of What Happens: Body and Education in the Making of Consciousness.* [online]. Hawthorne: EPDF.PUB. Available at: https://epdf.pub/queue/the-feeling-of-what-happens.html [Accessed 15 June 2019]

Hamlyn, D. W. 1988. *A History of Western Philosophy.* London: Pelican Books.

Norris, C. 1987. *Derrida.* London: Fontana Press.

Richter, D. J. no date. Ludwig Wittgenstein (1889–1951). [online]. *Internet Encyclopedia of Philosophy.* Available at: https://www.iep.utm.edu/wittgens/ [Accessed 15 June 2019]

Wittgenstein, L. 2001. *Philosophical Investigations.* Oxford: Blackwell Publishers.

Wittgenstein, L. 2010. Tractatus Logico-Philosophicus. [online]. Salt Lake City: Project Gutenberg. Available at: http://www.gutenberg.org/files/5740/5740-pdf.pdf [Accessed 15 June 2019].

III. FROM THE COUCH TO THE CLASSROOM

AN EXPLORATION OF THE POSSIBILITIES AND LIMITATIONS OF TRANSFERRING PRACTICES AND IDEAS FROM PSYCHOANALYSIS TO EDUCATIONAL CONTEXTS

> If you analyse the function of an object, its form often becomes obvious.
> — *Ferdinand Alexander Porsche, Grandson to the Engineer, Ferdinand Porsche*

As things stand, psychoanalysis seems to be one of the lesser-studied areas of research within the field of education. One could suppose, this is a consequence of either the highly-specialised nature of the discipline, its troubled history as a 'science' (Žižek, 2008: viii), or, perhaps, its *exclusive* use by educational psychologists seeking to help students with *particular* issues, but not in normal teaching. Whatever the cause, psychoanalysis nevertheless provides a feasible platform for healthy education and development. With that stated, the aim of this essay is to assess one such solution to a psychoanalytic inhibition through a broader analysis of the concept of the 'death drive' as elaborated by Sigmund Freud. The solution to be examined, especially, concerns 'mediating texts' (put simply, writing) by way of which, Julie Walsh proposes, pupils may obtain a certain amount of 'distance' (or personal space) in a tutorial setting with a teacher, and thereby cover or calm their anxiety when asked a question about verbally expressing a personal opinion. The conceptual link between the Walsh paper and the 'death drive' stems from Claudia Lapping's impression that Walsh's 'mediating texts' is a part-solution to the latter.

So sketched, after exploring the two above concepts, conclusions will be made through the critical insight of four unlikely authors into Freudian psychoanalysis: Carl Jung, Wilhelm Reich, Abraham Maslow, and Edward de Bono. Keeping in mind the philosophy of education as our primary 'lens', this selection is mainly due to the authors' direct relevance to our topic — and the opportunity to (re-)introduce their work to the field of contemporary education. To summarise, the four authors point out the weaknesses of the concept of the 'death drive' alongside Freudian 'techniques' and 'Psychoanalysis', as well as distinguish the highly significant difference between healthy and unhealthy individuals inside and outside the clinic. In this way, by drawing attention to the relevant overarching concepts of the 'death drive', 'analysis' and 'techniques', it becomes possible not only to evaluate the applicability of Freudian psychoanalysis on education, but to determine the practicality of Walsh's method as a psychoanalytic tool in education.

To that end, the three succeeding sections are structured in the following way. The first section explains Walsh's proposal for 'mediating texts' as a psychoanalytic technique. The second details the basics of Freudian psychoanalysis, alongside the 'death drive' and the application of that theory on education. The third, finally, assesses those concepts against the works of Jung, Reich, Maslow, and de Bono. Lastly, it must be noted, the educational *context* for this assessment primarily comprises the teacher-student interaction found in Julie Walsh's case study as described in the subsequent section.

Part I: 'Mediating Texts' as a Psychoanalytic Technique

Taken from a one-to-one encounter with a 19-year-old boy, Walsh's hypothesis, to be brief, revolves around the activity of 'mediating texts' (writing) as a psychoanalytic technique to calm anxiety when one is asked to respond orally to questions relating to personal opinions. In Walsh's case study, this is demonstrated by the subject's sense of self-consciousness, which prevents him from using language verbally upon being asked questions about his essay on Freud's ideas around sexuality (Walsh, 2014: 10f.). Therefore, Walsh stresses that while talking about this subject matter may be a cause for awkwardness, the difficulty in speaking could simply be a direct result of the act of speaking itself (ibid.: 11). In this regard, citing Žižek's issue with 'questions' as an instrument for the 'totalitarian intersubjective relationship' (Žižek in ibid.: 15), Walsh points out that 'questions', whatever their content or form, seem to bring out the impotence of the inquired without necessitating an answer at all. In this manner, the 'question form', as an intrusive tool, penetrates a person's defenses, lays it bare, and makes them vulnerable to an attack.[4]

In seeking a resolution to this matter, Walsh then presents the idea that speaking and writing have separate 'modes of engagement', through which each is affected by different types of anxiety (ibid.: 10). Indeed, comparing the dynamic in education with the one in therapy, she reveals that writing, as opposed to speaking, can be witnessed in the consulting room where patients communicate with their therapist by letter or e-mail before or after sessions (ibid.: 12). In this way, Walsh advocates, 'texts' in both education and therapy provide a 'neutral ground' upon which the stakeholders could focus on the actual issue, without having to make any eye contact (ibid.).

---

[4] Admittedly, there are distinct types of questions asked by educators in differing contexts (see, for example, Bridges, 1979: 115f.). Therefore, generalising about the nature of questions might overlook key differences in this regard between the couch and the classroom in practice — something that warrants consideration in future researches.

Fundamentally, that noted, this is based around Freud's idea of 'aloofness' (*Überlegenheit*) or distance. To contextualise, psychoanalysis originally began in the 'art of interpretation' — especially in acknowledging or realising unconscious material — but later developed into something of an active engagement with patients' 'resistances' in the unconscious (ibid.). Against this background, what remained unchanged was the analyst's attempt to give the patient a sense of 'aloofness' in order to ensure that the present experience was perceived by the patient as a repetition of a disparate situation in the past (ibid.). Walsh, as such, interprets 'aloofness' to mean distancing from 'transferential material' (anxiety transferred to the clinic and therapist from the past) as a necessary condition for the success of a psychoanalytic interpretation (ibid.: 14).

For all that, Walsh still questions, what if distancing failed to achieve its goal and, as a matter of course, brought shame to the subject anyway. Her reaction is that, contrary to first impressions, there are, in fact, positive consequences — incidentally two — in response to the feeling of being ashamed. The first, in short, is that it can clarify one's sense of 'proprietorship' and rights from those of others (ibid.: 17). The second is it can help reimagine the subject's 'subjectivity' or self-conception (ibid.). Ultimately, she explains, this is due to the fact that shame affects the enquirer too by exposing their weaknesses as well as impotence (ibid.: 15f.). In essence, simply put, shame blurs the boundaries of the self and other, facilitating the attainment of the two above-mentioned benefits. Here, by the way, the entirety of this perspective is aligned to Carl Jung's (1971: 31, 155) statement that psychiatry must be a 'dialogue between the sick psyche and the psyche of the doctor', whereby the latter is affected as equally as the former.

All in all, it is for this reason, and the possibility of writing 'mediating texts' basically, that questions can be a potential tool of psychoanalysis in education. As Maslow (1976: 14) once affirmed, it is sometimes crucial that in deciding 'what is best' for students, the most effective techniques must be devised to ease the communication of that information to us. In a sense, Walsh's proposal might be considered a unique contribution to this ideal, as it strives to overcome barriers in a learner's psyche. Be that as it may, to assess the potency of the foregoing idea, it is vital, next, that we undertake an analysis of Freudian psychoanalysis as well as the concept of the 'death drive'. The next section is in regard to this theme.

Part II: Freudian Psychoanalysis and the 'Death Drive'

To understand Freud's theory of the 'death drive', it is probably helpful, first of all, to review his initial conception of psychoanalysis and the techniques employed in it for that purpose. Beginning with the most central aspect, the human condition for Freud is largely shaped by the need for the gratification of pleasures or, quintessentially, the relaxation of 'an unpleasant state of tension' to avoid pain (Freud, 1922: 1). Expressly, he supported this claim by the evident function of dreams to produce pleasure through 'wish-fulfilments' (Freud, 1997: 34ff.). That is, at another level, he thought dreams represented the attempts of the 'unconscious' to adjust to one's mental and emotional environment, whilst failure resulted in psychotic or neurotic symptoms (ibid.: 9f.).

Generally speaking, the psychoanalysis of this denouement is explained in virtue of two interrelated features of the psyche. The first of these relates to the so-called 'conscious' and 'unconscious' processes. To elaborate, in a few words, the 'conscious' — as what we are aware of — consists of only the surface of a vast 'unconscious' realm — one that can neither be accessed nor searched for explicit content (Reich, 1970: 58). The middle barrier between these two domains, in its turn, is named the 'foreconscious', which not only defends the 'conscious' against the larger forces of the 'unconscious', but, sometimes when necessary, permits 'unconscious' content to surface in a disguised or symbolic form into the 'conscious'. Tentatively, suffused throughout this schema is another system, defined in terms of a conflict between the 'id' and 'superego'. Put simply, these forces encompass, *seriatim*, the primitive feelings and urges of individuals (which dwell in the 'unconscious') and the demands of society or civilisation imposed across the psyche ('conscious', 'foreconscious' and 'unconscious'). In this conflict, by the by, the balance is solicited by a third element of the psyche named the 'ego', whose operation is to prevent either the 'id' or 'superego' from overpowering the other in the 'conscious' (Freud, 1942: 10).

In this framework, congenitally, a healthy individual would demonstrate a unified 'ego' aware of its boundaries with the 'id' and 'superego' (Reich, 1970: 61), whereas an unhealthy individual would feel deeply distressed by the overwhelming material of the 'id' or 'superego', erupting, as it were, through the 'foreconscious' and into the 'conscious' ('ego'). On practical grounds, to prevent or treat the latter group, Freud corroborated the use of 'free associations' with reference to the interpretation of dreams as the object of attention. At the bottom, this connoted the communication of any thought that came to mind about a particular aspect of a dream, without omission of any thought whatsoever, even if it appeared trivial at a glance. Indeed, the instant this course of treatment is performed, the patient is expected to become aware (or 'consciously' acknowledge) of the origin of his or her imbalance, at what stage the negative symptoms would begin to disappear spontaneously. 'Transference', in this setting, springs from the given opportunity (in the treatment room) to the patient to externalise their distress on to the therapist in furtherance of a clearer interpretation (Lapping, 2019: 3).

Despite everything heretofore, the publication of *Beyond the Pleasure Principle* substantially altered Freudian psychoanalysis by dint of integrating the concept of the 'death drive' into the overall frame of reference (Freud, 1922: 4). In basic terms, the 'death drive' refers to an innate urge compelling the return of mankind toward some sort of an earlier condition, probably along the lines of death (ibid.: 44). In this spirit, contrasting the 'death drive' to the above-described pleasure ('sexual') instinct, Freud not only comes to doubt the origin of the latter, but alleges that its import is effectively secondary to the 'death' instinct; and appears, at the very most, to be a result of external factors conducing organisms to greater reproduction and variety, besides increasing complexity (ibid.: 47f.). In summary, beholding the living substance in terms of a double system, 'Eros' ('sexual' instinct) and 'Thanatos' ('death drive'), he judged the former the living force uniting and expanding life — albeit, with turbulence and tension; the latter the overarching instinct compelling life into nothingness (Reich, 1970: 136).

Practically speaking, the 'death drive' engenders what Freud called the 'compulsion to repeat'. In this connection, there is an unconscious need for punishment and, to that extent, an intrinsic inhibition against therapy or a healthy lifestyle (Reich, 1970: 136). To illustrate, Freud disclosed the case of an eighteen-months-old child who never cried when his mother left for several hours before returning home (Freud, 1922: 12). In this instance, the child frequently played a game akin to the departure and return of the mother, whereupon pleasure was procured in the latter phase (ibid.: 13). Yet, what is interesting, the child readily played the first part of the game, involving the disappearance (pain), more often than the latter part, involving the return (pleasure) (ibid.: 13f.). Admittedly, although Freud imagined that this could have been a product of the 'power' instinct ('mastery of a situation'), he proposed that the 'death drive' — in the form of 'revenge' — was dominant in the child's behaviour and, what is worse, persisted as a 'repeated' phenomenon (ibid.: 14ff.). For all these reasons, Freud concluded humans were ultimately destined to commit 'self-destructive' behaviours (ibid.: 17f.). As such, even the other possible instincts suspected — for example, 'self-preservation' – were only part-instincts whose real function was to lead to death ('inorganic order') (ibid.: 48).

On balance, that said, applying the concept of the 'death drive' to an educational setting, Claudia Lapping proclaims Freudian psychoanalysis as a substantive device to explore conditions underlying the human psyche and, therewith, preclude or treat what may be described as situational repressions ('compulsion to repeat') in all spheres of praxis and theory belonging to education. Doubtless, in this sense, Lapping views Walsh's aforesaid proposal ('mediating texts') as one of the solutions in which psychoanalysis could be employed for resolving inhibitions (like anxiety) in education. Hitherto, our inquiry has summed up an overview of Walsh's 'mediating texts' (as a psychoanalytic technique), Freudian psychoanalysis, and the concept of the 'death drive'. The following section broadly assesses the preceding considerations against the observations of four psychoanalysts who, somehow, have been affiliated with Freudian psychoanalysis.

Part III: Assessing 'Mediating Texts' — Its Theory and Practice

This section focuses on two aspects of Walsh's proposal: the viability of the concept of the 'death drive' upon which Walsh has based her 'mediating texts'; next, the practical efficacy of this psychoanalytic instrument in a classroom. The educational contexts in consideration include Walsh's one-to-one engagement, and, to a lesser extent, whole classes.

To begin with, according to Wilhelm Reich (one of Freud's second-generation students), the 'death drive' emerged, historically speaking, in reaction to colleagues who had labelled Freud a 'charlatan' and threatened the general self-preservation and progress of a medical movement, which he had wholly found in the early 1890s (Reich, 1970: 138, 215). The concept of a 'death drive', as such, was something of a compromise — by rejecting 'pleasure' as the prior instinct — in order to offset the declining reputation of Psychoanalysis. Obviously, there may well be more to this story than meets the eye. Nonetheless, the concept of a 'death drive' does not entirely hold together as it stands.

For starters, Freud could not explain the origin of the — opposing — pleasure ('sexual') instinct, regardless of his detailed survey into cell division. In short, Freud observed whereas some organisms altered due to pressure from external influences, others survived through reproduction and cell division (Freud, 1922: 49). Parenthetically, he viewed the lifelong process in the form of two distinct cells, 'soma' (which approach death) and 'germ' (which approach immortality) (ibid.: 56). Then, he pointed out, that some experiments had evinced that successive generations lost vitality and perished if they were not invigorated some way (ibid.: 60). In contradistinction, later, he reported other experiments had revealed opposing results. In tandem, he also speculated the above findings applied only to multicellular, not unicellular, organisms as the latter were composed of a single cell, in possession of both 'soma' and 'germ' qualities (ibid.: 57). However, when he reached his final reflection, he treated the 'death drive' in an unmistakably ambiguous tone. In sum, he was not just unclear about the origin of the 'sexual' (pleasure) instinct, but decided to mark the primacy of the 'death drive' as mere speculation — rather than conviction — that had to be proven wrong, first and main.

Altogether, although the theoretical scheme (i.e. 'death drive') on which Walsh and Lapping have grounded their argument may be suspicious, it would be another mistake to establish a middle way, as Lapping appears to do, by confirming Freud's concept of the 'death drive' as 'neither true nor false' (Lapping, 2019: 7). To wit, according to Freud's theory, this is due to the notion that there is always a dominant instinct that remains absolutely above all others. In which instance, the question is which of the two — the 'death drive' or the 'pleasure-principle' — is the most logical. In response, it may be appropriate to slightly alter Lapping's cited position. Therefore, both possibilities call for an analysis of their particular implications.

To that end, on the one hand, if the 'death drive' is found the dominant instinct, any type of therapy or treatment would be purely worthless since the outcome is nothing but 'death' and 'self-destruction'. All meaning, if one could not cure a patient, the 'death instinct' would be conveniently blamed as the determining biological striving (Reich, 1970: 137): therefore, when people commit murder, it is because they want to go to prison; when children steal, it is to obtain relief from a conscience (ibid.). On the other hand, howbeit, if the 'pleasure-principle' is presumed the dominant instinct, the 'death drive' would need to be 'demoted' to one of several 'part-instincts' — e.g. 'power' and 'self-preservation' instincts. In this light, the ramification on Lapping's (and, for what it is worth, Walsh's) proposal is clear. The concept of the 'death drive' (and 'mediating texts') can only remain relevant if it is considered a 'part-instinct' — instead of an unstoppable 'compulsion to repeat' — that can be manipulated or availed toward a superior education system. All this implies, even though the critique above does not upset the practice of 'mediating texts' as an instrument of psychoanalysis per se, it insists the theoretical framework (i.e. 'death drive') buttressing its function is rethought in an effort to secure its conceptual coherence and prevent misapprehensions of the ideal for allied developments in the offing.

Moving onward to a blind spot in the conceptual framework behind 'mediating texts', the tacit comparative thus far betwixt therapists and patients in the consultancy room with teachers and students in the classroom is possibly presumptive. Crucially, the adaptation of psychoanalysis for education seems to bear the assumption that psychoanalysis can be reemployed in other areas of society, *mutatis mutandis*. However, let us take cognisance of the people found in clinics and schools: whilst one accommodates healthy individuals, the other receives the mentally unhealthy. In this way, illustratively, Abraham Maslow's study of 'self-actualised' people and their potentials showcases that different sectors of society contain people of varied capabilities, mental health, and above all personal requirements (Maslow, 1976: 7). One must, therefore, take care not to treat every individual like a 'bag of symptoms' (ibid.). In which case, naturally, sweeping statements about the use of (Freudian) psychoanalytic tools on, so to speak, healthy students in schools must be clarified beforehand as researchers in education (like Walsh) develop psychoanalytic techniques for the sake of policy and practice.

It is obviously beyond the scope of this paper to pursue the above study much further. So, shifting focus to the *practice* of 'mediating texts' (while presuming psychoanalysis *can* be implemented in education), Freudian psychoanalysis certifies that the proper function of therapists, principally, is to gain insight into the history, urges, tensions and activities (not symptoms) of patients on account of the broader premise that one's 'character armour' is virtually the net impact of all repressions imposed in the past (Maslow, 1976: 14; additionally, see above on the interpretation of dreams and 'free association'). Without this information, one way or another, therapy cannot really begin (Jung, 1971: 138). In accordance thereof, effective therapy should emanate only from the operation of managing the patient's 'whole being' and resolving their 'character resistances' (ibid.: 147).

So said, whether this motion applies to 'mediating texts' is somewhat questionable, because the idea of 'aloofness' (distancing) by way of writing seems to elude psychological repressions within. By way of illustration, it is possible patients may not cooperate with the analyst by telling them what they want, or expect to hear. Alternatively, in more difficult cases, patients might be so inhibited they either cannot write anything, or do not want to write anything (Reich, 1970: 67). Sometimes, even, there is a possibility of 'latent hostility' and resistance towards the analyst (ibid.: 129). It is hard to say, in these circumstances, how 'mediating texts' can resolve repression by calming or covering anxiety, as opposed to addressing the root of the issue head-on. In the end, 'aloofness' (distancing) works provided there is transference *vis-à-vis* the source of repression, not the content of an essay as explicitly intended with the use of 'mediating texts'.

Relevantly, it could also be argued, writing (as a medium) limits 'free association' due to the general tendency to write 'formally' — which disguises, if not contorts, emotions and feelings — when voicing thoughts (de Bono, 1987: 211). Furthermore, even if writing *has* some potential as a pertinent method, Walsh is none the wiser about the precise form of a written text. Certainly, the apparent choice is probably the essay form, even though it is likely to involve an argument in support of a case (introduction, key points, etc.), and have a 'too laboured' construction aside (ibid.: 212).

As a whole, in connection with the aforesaid, two counterpoints may be made in defence of 'mediating texts'. The first concerns the alleged lack of attention regarding the actual *practice* of psychoanalysis through psychoanalytic techniques. According to Reich (1970: 66), this is possibly why Freud did not exhibit many successful therapies himself. What is more, recalling the above account on the significance of personal histories and 'character armours', it would go without stating individuals have different therapeutic needs and requirements on every single occasion. Apropos to this, psychotherapists must never rely on any single technique or interpretation, for there is no universal solution that can be applied to all cases (Jung, 1971: 153). It would, therefore, seem Walsh's technique, as a proposed psychoanalytic instrument, provides another tool within the psychoanalyst's 'toolbox' in therapy sessions (needless to mention, the teacher's application of psychoanalysis in a classroom). The only caveat, in this instance, is that 'mediating texts' must be treated as a *single* tool solely, not as an all-embracing tool. At the end of the day, even silence — as a 'manner' of communication — can express something which could be understood over a period of time (Reich, 1970: 176). Bypassing silence through writing ('mediating texts') is not, thus, the right therapeutic solution at all times. When this criticism is taken into account, only then can one admit the significance of 'character' has been fully accommodated into psychotherapy (and teaching) as the determining criterion.

Second, in defence of the form of 'mediating texts', it should be noted there are other alternatives that could significantly minimise the 'formality' of written texts. In particular, the two most obvious that spring to mind include the list form (i.e. bullet points) and the note form. According to de Bono, these formats could make the separation, assessment, and sorting of ideas easier for the reader (therapist and teacher), while the writer can focus on the ideas themselves, rather than the connections between sentences (de Bono, 1987: 212). For younger people, in contrast, one possibility is something like boxes or headings under which suitable material could be written down (ibid.). This would allow the patients (or students) to organise their thoughts spontaneously without needing to filter individual thought content. What these examples indicate, all in all, is writing through 'mediating texts' (as a substitute for speaking) might not be as constricting as initially recognised if the appropriate formats are selected depending upon the context.

All things considered, having placed 'mediating texts' in a theoretical and practical context, the preceding arguments demonstrate that while the concept of a 'death drive' and the practice of 'mediating texts' have their particular shortcomings, these must be adapted, in turn, for appropriate use in education. Hence, while the concept of the 'death drive' is demoted to a 'part-instinct', 'mediating texts' must be treated as a single tool amidst other psychoanalytic tools and implemented accordingly.

Conclusion

On the whole, Lapping believes psychoanalysis has pertinent lessons for education (Lapping, 2019: 7). In particular, her contention is that as a 'site of transference', the role of teachers and policymakers in education is to clarify and, most importantly, resolve repetitious patterns (ibid.: 10). Thereto, those in education must be open to experimentation and to using different techniques (ibid.: 11). As it happens, Walsh's idea of 'mediating texts' as a tool for 'aloofness' (distancing), based on the Freudian premise and the 'death drive', can be a useful psychoanalytic technique within the context of the observations made in this essay. Here, it is worth noting, that there has been no academic work regarding Walsh's 'mediating texts', analysing, let alone assessing, its use as a psychoanalytic instrument. Thus, the overall contribution of this paper to the current literature on psychoanalysis and education consists in its assessment of 'mediating texts' within a broader context of Freudian psychoanalysis and the concept of the 'death drive'.

In this endeavour, it is concluded that 'mediating texts' can offer a useful instrument as long as the following are borne in mind: first, the concept of the 'death drive' is most likely a 'part-instinct' rather than the primary biological drive; second, although writing is not intended to tackle the source of anxiety (in speaking) head-on, it may nonetheless work on some individuals, depending on their personal history and repressions, as one psychoanalytic technique amidst others; third, 'mediating texts' are probably only effective if the writing is undertaken in either list form or note form. Lastly, as a subject for future discussion, it was recommended to closely analyse the telling applicability of psychoanalysis as a medical movement to the field of education. To conclude, there is clearly more to be expected from this area, particularly in view of the fact some psychoanalysts such as Jung, Reich, and Maslow have not been seriously reviewed in these circles. In view of this anticipation, what is most significant for future researches is to ensure that the theoretical framework is coherent throughout. Hopefully, this essay has taken a step in emphasising the necessity of this approach.

BIBLIOGRAPHY

De Bono, E. 1987. *Teaching Thinking*. London: Penguin Books.

Bridges, D. 1979. *Education, Democracy and Discussion*. Slough: NFER.

Freud, S. 1922. *Beyond the Pleasure Principle*. London: The International Psycho-Analytical Press.

Freud, S. 1942. *Totem and Taboo*. Middlesex: Penguin Books.

Freud, S. 1997. *The Interpretation of Dreams*. Hertfordshire: Wordsworth Editions.

Jung, C. G. 1971. *Memories, Dreams, Reflections*. London: Collins.

Lapping, C. 2019. Introduction: The death drive and education. In: C. Lapping, ed. *Freud, Lacan, Zizek and Education*. London: Routledge, pp. 1-11.

Maslow, A. H. 1976. *The Farther Reaches of Human Nature*. Middlesex: Penguin Books.

Reich, W. 1970. *The Function of the Orgasm*. London: Panther Books.

Walsh, J. 2014. 'Interrupting the frame: reflective practice in the classroom and the consulting room'. *Pedagogy, Culture & Society* 22

(1), pp. 9-19.

Žižek, S. 2008. *The Sublime Object of Ideology*. London: Verso.

IV. OF THE RIGHT OF PRISONERS TO EDUCATION

FROM READINGS ON CLASSICAL LIBERALS, KANT AND FOUCAULT

> Those who submit — as the majority does — are conditioned to a life lived without their human birthright: work done with the joy and creativity of love.
> — *Marjorie Spock, Environmentalist, Author, and Poet*

The right of prisoners to education is pronounced by multiple international laws and conventions presently in force. Examples include the Universal Declaration of Human Rights, 1952 European Convention for the Protection of Human Rights and Fundamental Freedoms, as well as the Charter of Fundamental Rights of the European Union — each continuing to uphold prisoners' right to education as human beings. However, the right to education is far from notionally straightforward as it might appear, given the fact governments around the world have yet to implement (fully) the terms of these international agreements. This chapter seeks to evaluate whether or not prison populations should have the right to education — as a rule — from the points of view of three schools of philosophy: Utilitarianism/Kantianism, in the first and second sections, and Foucault's largely undervalued socio-political interpretation of the function of prisons in the third part. Utilitarianism/Kantianism are anticipated as basic points of departure in any debate about the right of prisoners to education, whereas Foucault's reflections introduce a further level of depth to the present literature. Conclusively, it is affirmed Kant's defence of prisoners' right to education is more convincing than the Utilitarian justification, despite the former case's somewhat problematic ambiguity in its practical application. Furthermore, it is affirmed the socio-political structures that suffuse the operations of prisons should not be treated separately to matters discussed in theory, since day-to-day matters of praxis in prisons unknowingly diminish individual rights.

Understandably, we are focusing on the philosophical bases of the claim to education, instead of analyses on legality; for good measure, although education can take a variety of distinctive forms, from family to church to mass media, we will regard education solely in its traditional form, that is to say, one that incorporates elements of human contrivance or design to transfer and acquire knowledge, values, and attitudes (Darkenwald and Merriam, 1982: 2, 6). Equally, that said, we will not address certain debates about adult education, adulthood, and learning. After all, this field of inquiry is still in its adolescence (ibid.: 39, 229).

Part I: 'Utility' of Schooling Prisoners

Contextually, although *individual* rights are rooted in Kantianism, whereas Utilitarianism is concerned with *overall* 'utility' (usefulness or good) for the greatest number, we will assume for the purpose of this discussion that if the agenda to educate imprisoned persons is *overall* expedient, then Utilitarians would have a legitimate reason to establish this activity as a 'right'. Parenthetically, before delving into the 'utility' of educating prisoners, it is worth evoking classical liberal statements about liberty, learning, and the purpose of prisons as useful points of reference in order to clarify the underlying nexus between Utilitarianism and the education of prisoners.

A Utilitarian, John Stuart Mill (1806–1873), believed all human beings must have certain fundamental liberties to author their lives without impairing the entitlements of others at any time (Mill, 1991: 14). Simply, everyone should be permitted to reign over their actions (ibid.) and be able to protect themselves and others, or acquire something in compensation for any act of injustice (Locke in Nozick, 2013: 10). Otherwise, they ought to hold the right to punish offenders in so far as to impede any violations of their rights in the future. But, in view of the fact a few inconveniences (such as force, fraud, and theft) are inevitable in a 'state of nature', traditional liberals championed the mediation of a dominant third party (in the form of a civil government) to settle matters betwixt inhabitants fairly and reliably, shorn of the slightest misuse of power to populace's detriment (Locke in ibid.: 10ff.). For this purpose, while an ideal government is equipped to utilise coercion to endorse self-determination and safeguard private interests from outside intrusion, its procedures have got to be constricted to nothing more than those found in what is now called a 'night-watchman' state (Nagel, 2013: xiv; Mill, 1991: 7, 14; Nozick, 2013: xix). Only this prerequisite guarantees, perchance, unrestricted conversation in search of the truth, in keeping with Mill's notions of progress and teleology (Mill, 1991: 25; Gray, 1991: ix).

Really, the Old Liberals reasoned, independence necessitates that one be trained and tutored in accordance with one's inimitable and miscellaneous requirements (Mill, 1991: 64, 117). If not, they wind up being like others, and participation in government loses its potential democratic quality (ibid.: 117; Haywood, 1994: 174). Mainly, schooling is constructive for the reason that it cultivates the intellect, individual self-actualisation, personal and social improvement, as well as social transformation or organisational effectiveness (Darkenwald and Merriam, 1982: 42ff.). Bearing in mind the analysis that tutelage can be more helpful than damaging, it is time to inspect how Utilitarianism may uphold criminals' right to education.

Specifically, for Utilitarians, education has social, economic, or personal benefits both for prisoners as well as the society within which they live (Vorhaus, 2014: 162). Concurrently, for example, education may increase a detainee's chances of being employed or re-integrating into their society (Coates, 2016: i-ii) — on the assumption, of course, that the detained person has low levels of literacy and numeracy alongside the presupposition that employment in labour markets is only possible through acquired qualifications (Vorhaus, 2014: 165). Thereupon, employment not only gives an offender a means to gain a sense of belonging in their community as a compatriot (Department for Business, Innovation, and Skills in ibid.: 165), it lessens incidents of re-offence and even saves finances — from £2,000 to £28,000 per offender, as reported by a study in the United Kingdom (ibid.: 166). Also, after a 'period of incarceration' (Laub and Sampson, 2001: 58), education may supply an absorbing experience in proportion to the necessities, characteristics, and aspirations of each individual (Vorhaus, 2014: 165), not to mention encourage convicts to take control of their lives and boost their self-esteem out of (depressing) sentiences of 'failure' toward gaining substance or merit (Darkenwald and Merriam in ibid.). Optimally, even if an ex-criminal is not immediately hired by an employer, they will have enough self-sufficiency and self-respect to persevere and aspire.

Conversely, sure enough, there are sundry flaws regarding the aforesaid vindications. One that speedily springs to mind is that it is somewhat challenging to certify those assertions thanks to shortcomings 'in scope, specificity and methodological rigor' in measuring outcome performances (Vorhaus, 2014: 162, 165). Surely, to be branded a criminal in official records typically weakens one's odds in securing a job (Fletcher et al. in ibid.: 165); a case in point, a former inmate in England found work as a lecturer in a university after roughly 800 attempts (see Warr, no date). Moreover, it is not always clear if either 'rehabilitation' or 'retribution' (deterrence) is the prime objective of education (Vorhaus, 2014: 166). In reality, if compulsory education is intended to be part of a convict's punishments, then there is no reason for education to rehabilitate (ibid.): concomitantly, whatever is taught by force will weaken its benefits by compromising a prisoner's self-confidence and motivation (ibid.: 167). Within the limits of broader public prejudices, at this point, one is bound to suspect how prison populations can profit from being taught.

Anyway, the most critical comment follows from Immanuel Kant (1724–1804). Briefly, if certain 'utilities', like happiness, welfare, or self-preservation for the greatest number truly embodied the very core of our human race, it would prove much easier and more precise if instinct, which innately seeks these values, took sole charge of the body, prescribed every action and excluded, in unison, any intervention on the part of reason or mind (Kant, 1993b: 8). For Kant, Utilitarianism is not able to decide consistently and accurately what ends it strives to achieve at all times (ibid.: 27), due to the fact any Utilitarian value is an 'empirical' concept (derived from experience) affected by variable conditions in both the present and future (ibid.); so, even if one tried to satisfy higher pleasures, say, long-term happiness by way of reason (as maintained by Mill), instead of basic needs, it is 'experience' that is cultivated and not rationality: essentially, the cause of higher pleasures belongs to the (lower) faculty of senses, which are changeable eternally (Kant, 1993a: 22f.).

Stated so, the right of prisoners to education, as far as Kant's critique of Utilitarianism is concerned, becomes superfluous since the latter philosophical system theoretically excludes from the equation the higher faculty of 'reason' whenever and wherever it attempts to determine goals and means. Avowedly, Utilitarianism sustains limited credibility in supporting the proposition that education has clear advantages for people in — or, for that matter, outside — prisons. Henceforward, the segment succeeding sets out an alternative defence of the right of those in prisons to education that is perhaps more convincing than its Utilitarian counterpart discussed hitherto.

Part II: Kantian Ethics on the Right of Prisoners to Education

Whilst Robert Nozick (1938–2002) reiterated certain Enlightenment values and ideas centred on individual liberties (that at the time of his book, *Anarchy, State and Utopia,* 1974) were half-neglected — particularly in the wake of John Rawls' predominance as a moral and political philosopher — it is nevertheless Kant's system of thought that postulates an original logic for the rights of individual human beings. (The notional weaknesses that underpin Utilitarianism was something Nozick did not verbalise himself, mayhap, because he was engaged in using examples to 'prove' an argument — as he declared himself — instead of scrutinising deeper-seated conceptual matters.) Wherefore, *inter alia*, this section — broadly — draws upon Kant's major piece on philosophy, *Critique of Pure Reason*, and his famous texts on morality, *Grounding for the Metaphysics of Morals* and *Critique of Practical Reason*, to lay the basis for and, subsequently, assess the right of prisoners to education. The latter works, it hardly needs to be stressed, sought to attend to every field of morals (including politics and education), very much like Plato's Chief Good or Aristotle's Prime Mover (Ellington, 1993: v).

To understand Kant's *Morals*, it is important at the outset to describe his metaphysics. Shortly, in his first *Critique*, Kant endorsed the synthetic unity of apperception as the highest aim for the whole of general logic, employment of the understanding, and transcendental philosophy. Simplistically, Kant aimed to draw a wedge between 'rationalism' and 'empiricism' (Hamlyn, 1988: 218), so that one would treat right and wrong *not* in the sense of 'a single homogenising standard' of outcomes (Nagel, 2013: xii) as in Utilitarianism, but in reference to the dictates of 'reason' (Ellington, 1993: vi). Generally, Kant presupposed that reason stems from a congenital split between *a priori* (independently of experience) and empirical (derived from experience or *a posteriori*) faculties in the human organism (ibid.: ix). Consecutively, to join the two, he professed knowledge instigates from experience but does not arise from it (Hamlyn, 1988: 218). That is to say, cognition awakens once objects are registered by the senses by means of the operation of two different forms of sensuous intuition, one internal (time) and the other external (space), as representations ('*phenomena*') of 'things-in-themselves' ('*noumena*') (ibid.: 220; Kant, 2018: 1, 21ff.; 1993b: 52). Precisely, the *a priori* faculty turns raw material of the senses into the knowledge of the world outside (Kant, 2018: 1) by organising experiences into categories and concepts formed *a priori* — according to two indispensable preconditions — 'necessity' and 'universality' (Hamlyn, 1988: 218) — each of which is essential to his moral philosophy (Kant, 2018: 2ff.).[5]

Kant anticipated that though one knows *a priori* he or she is free, it is not viable to fully apprehend how this is feasible, given the fact the entirety of one's cognitive faculties are limited and cannot go beyond a specified point — into *noumena* (Kant, 1993a: 16; Beck, 1993: x). For Kant, thus, claims around speculative metaphysics (for instance, God is real or Will is free) could never be discussed (Beck, 1993: xiv, xvi). Our in-born ability to think and act rationally implies we are to perform moral duties — unlike animals, which act wholly upon instincts and sensuous inclinations (ibid.: xi). Therewith, freedom connotes grasping moral laws stipulated *a priori* as well as performing them as a matter of duty (Kant, 1993a: 5, 30).

Conjoining his *Morals* (Beck, 1993: xf.), Kant proposed that 'practical' reason translates into reality what is already contrived *in abstracto* (Kant, 1993a: 70; 1993b: 3). Generically, 'practical' reason synthesises (bridges) *a priori* and empirical faculties and, in so doing, concedes a two-way process (induction and deduction) between the two, which results in a (supposed) 'unity of theory and practice' (Critchley, 2001: 19). Quintessentially, 'practical' reason applies moral laws acquired *a priori* from the formulations of the 'Categorical Imperative' to actuality.

Meanwhile, the ensuing sentence best summarises the first formulation of the composition of the 'Categorical Imperative'

---

[5] Famously, the following statement exemplifies the complementary nature of the two faculties: 'Thoughts without content are empty, intentions without concepts are blind' (Kant in Hamlyn, 1988: 219).

— as Kant's overarching moral tenet: 'Always act in such a way that you can also will that the maxim of your action should become a universal law' (Kant in Ellington, 1993: v). Simply, an agent who perpetrates a wrong act must be willing to accept identical treatment towards themselves someday (ibid.: vii). Tellingly, a lie is principally self-defeating as it loses its efficacy the moment others begin to follow suit (ibid.); in other words, to procure success, a liar must be able to take exception to an 'imperative' followed by everybody else (ibid.). Comparatively, self-murder to preclude potential acts of evil on others (Kant, 1993b: 30f.) is contradictory per se because what is deemed universal must — by definition — bear upon one's self indiscriminately (ibid.: 31). Summarily, a maxim — no matter its content — is a ruling that must be obeyed all the time in aims, means, and circumstances, absolutely (Ellington, 1993: vi-vii).

Secondarily, the 'Categorical Imperative' particularises, 'one should always act in such a way that humanity either in oneself or in others is always treated as an end in itself and never merely as a means' (Kant, 1993b: 40). Wherefore, if people are treated as an instrument, they have no purpose — or autonomy — of their own as rational organisms (Ellington, 1993: vii); indeed, autonomy rests at the heart of this formulation (ibid.: vi), and it demands that human beings must not be treated as 'objects' or 'non-humans' (Vorhaus, 2014: 170): characteristically, to be autonomous, a being must be able to 'act as a law unto [itself]' by virtue of its rationality — i.e. as a co-author or legislator (Ellington, 1993: vi-vii); for, once push comes to shove, each individual is equal to another by dint of being human. When autonomy culminates society-wide, there will emerge a 'kingdom of ends' composed of people who — as free and equal members of society — respect and further the ends of their fellow citizens (ibid.: vi). Hereafter, this 'kingdom of ends' represents a community where each member legislates universal laws and becomes subject to those laws unequivocally.

Frankly, Kant deemed several moral 'imperatives' had to be followed by every human being as a matter of 'duty' — e.g. preserving one's life, honouring contracts, not overindulging in food and drink, developing all-natural faculties and talents (ibid.: xi; Kant, 1993b: 31). Conventionally, Kantians say '[education] is an imperative in its own right' and that the current criminal justice environment stresses jailed peoples' wrongs in the stead of 'their humanity, their potential, and their human rights' (Muñoz in Vorhaus, 2014: 168). Whence, in spite of the fact prisoners do not necessarily have physical liberty (as a matter of 'justice', see Kant, 1993a: 39), they must enjoy the right to education, not just as individuals universally curious to know and understand our world better, but as ends-in-themselves who bear personal autonomy (Vorhaus, 2014: 162, 168).

Distinctly, there are three grounds for a prisoner's 'human right' (personal autonomy's legal offshoot) to education: 'dignity, respect for persons, and citizenship' (ibid: 169). Firstly, 'dignity' refers to something that is above price, unlike whatever that has a price or can be exchanged for anything comparable (Kant, 1993b: 40). (Certainly, 'dignity' is incompatible with punishment and torture of any type because it unavoidably harms a victim's standing as an end; Kant, 1993b: 41.) Secondly, each individual has the right to be 'treated' with 'respect' as equal fellow human beings. All intimating, under no circumstances whatsoever should one overlook the inference that each human is on a par with another by reason of being human. Thirdly, every personage owns the right to join or re-integrate into society ('kingdom of ends') as active citizens (Vorhaus, 2014: 169). Judiciously, the most important substructure for a 'human right' to education is 'human dignity' owing to the fact it implies respect for an individual in their 'actuality' — plus, education gives rise to holistic development, enhances learning, and fulfils potential (Muñoz in ibid.: 169).

Howbeit, the choice between the right of an inmate to education as 'universal' or 'inalienable' is vague and slightly confusing (ibid.: 169ff.). Obliquely, it is uncertain if the *general* right to education should apply to prisoners too, nor what is strictly required if it is. Cordially, it could be asked if a victim does not acquire an absolute right to penalise a criminal, especially since Kant highlighted the significance of justice and enforcing contracts between two (or more) parties. Rather quizzically, there is uncertainty about whether those who violate other persons' liberties forfeit their own basic rights (Vorhaus, 2014: 162); or that education is an 'inalienable' right that cannot be forsaken or removed due to bad behaviour (ibid.: 169). Sometimes, after all, classes preclude a crime and preserve the safety of those inside a prison: as ends-in-themselves (ibid.: 164).[6] Apparently, Bertrand Russell (1947: 738) noted, '[i]f taken seriously, it [Kantianism] would make it impossible to reach a decision whenever two people's interests conflict'. Be that as it may, certainty *vis-à-vis* criminals' right to education as 'universal' or 'inalienable' is warranted before Kant's moral beliefs are considered effectual or applicable.

Regardless, 'dignity' may be unintentionally disrespected on some peculiar occasions (ibid.: 170). Allegorically, convicts who possess high levels of literacy and numeracy may perceive enforced learning as an insult if they were inserted into basic (albeit well-intended) courses (ibid.). Anyhow, what represents 'dignity' varies according to a person's self-appraisal together with the milieus whereabout one finds oneself (McCrudden in ibid.: 171). Clearly, in incongruous settings, people will be involuntarily vulnerable to a sense of self-hatred, loss of self-respect and dignity (ibid.); all suggesting, it is not evident what 'dignity' points at when it attempts to define the groundwork in line with prisoners' 'human right' to education (ibid.). Observably, it is usually emphasised torture or other degrading treatments alike violate 'dignity' (ibid.). But, then again, this does not illuminate what actions or capacities ensure 'dignity' or who has 'dignity'. Relevantly, to be sure, one of Russell's overarching observations is, '[t]o get a sufficient criterion [about what must constitute rights], we should have to abandon Kant's purely formal point of view, and take some account of the effects of actions' (Russell, 1947: 738). Presumably, as Critchley (2001: 86) argued, Kantianism lacks a unifying standard that combines theory with practice, a duality quite noticeably spotted in what he termed 'antinomies'. Qualifiedly, 'practical' reason does not resolve

---

[6] Overall, this resembles voting privileges in different countries according to one's age (Vorhaus, 2014: 169).

this dilemma, as it bridges faculties in the mind, but does not unify dualities — as it is extraordinarily distinguished in Hegel's Synthesis, Heidegger's Being, or Nietzsche's Will.

Factually, to sum up, Kant's fixation on the theory of his philosophy, but not its exercise, presents a hardship in bringing about a strong resolution. To inquire further, we revealed prisoners' entitlement to tutorial lessons with reference to 'universality' or 'inalienability' (or both) is ambiguous. Therewith, we decided 'dignity' or the status of every person as an end-in-themselves is inexact, since each may be swayed by one's self-perception and circumstances; besides, there are no discernible links with praxis. Wherefore, it is not wholly self-evident that Kant's position is correct and, if it is, how to defend it. Yet, this does not push aside Kant's defence of prisoners' right to education, particularly when made in relation to theoretical and practical weaknesses found within Utilitarianism. Zealously, all matters considered, as a 'universal' law and a means to treat folks as ends-in-themselves (in keeping with the 'Categorical Imperative' and its assorted specifications), Kant advances a convincing defence of the right of prisoners to education — at this point.

Part III: Foucault, Power, and Prisons

Wistfully, Michel Foucault (1926–1984) mistrusts 'power' and its leverage contra 'rationality'. Contextually, Johann Georg Hamann (one of Kant's early critics; 1730–1788) argued if 'reason' can criticise everything, then it must be able to criticise itself; an observation that finally led to nihilism and a number of unifying principles, such as Nietzsche's Will, alluded to earlier (Critchley, 2001: 31). Unduly, this line of thought reincarnated later in Michel Foucault's penetrating insights into the enterprise of prisons (ibid.: 16); after all, public institutions' intrinsic benevolence must not be taken for granted; in which case, it may be helpful to set out the origin of prisons in the first place.

Firstly, Foucault protested that the underlying intent of key institutions in society — army, police, hospitals, schools, prisons et al. — is structural 'control' (or management) of populations; in other words, prisons are not really created to reintegrate criminals into society (i.e. rehabilitation), but to exercise 'power' and dominance: in a sense, Foucault (1991: 128, 138f.) propounded that institutional coercion — in the form of discipline of the most detailed aspects of human behaviour — produces obedient subjects that show distinctive pre-determined 'habits, rules, orders'. Likewise, education is a means to 'control' individuals inside prisons. Unashamedly, from this standpoint, penal systems (alongside other institutions, e.g. asylums and schools) are designed *not* to give autonomy or rehabilitate incarcerated persons, but to impose discipline: for Foucault, this was a development that could be traced across history to public tortures and executions, which were employed to inflict fear in peoples' hearts (as popular spectacles) and ensure they followed prevalent social instructions without any real capacity to question structural power or knowledge — affected from above by those in positions of authority (ibid.: ix);[7] undoubtedly, if we assume, as Foucault did, that this is still the underlying socio-political function of prisons, or for that matter education, both 'rehabilitation' and

---

[7] Momentarily, the following account outlines the history of punishment. Originally, punishment was carried out by way of public tortures and executions displayed as popular spectacles (Foucault, 1991: ix); afterwards, under Napoleon Bonaparte's emerging 'nation-state', these deep-rooted customs appeared obsolete and were replaced by modern manifestations and arrangements that distributed power away from concentrated points (*videlicet* monarch and executioner) to public institutions (ibid.: 7, 80). Manifestly, these 'humanising' processes subtly aimed to support hugely complex apparatuses that disguised modern penal systems and, simultaneously, resolved elites' worries about social disturbances or feelings of solidarity during bloody executions (ibid.: 9, 61ff.): that is to say, discipline in prisons took priority and consisted of three features — enclosure by high walls, portioned personal spaces, and functional sites (ibid.: 141ff.). Observably, 'panopticism' took precedence in relation to rewards and punishments (ibid.: 170, 181) by targeting the soul, as opposed to the body as the 'focal' point, through long-term supervisions of behaviour and understanding causal processes behind illicit acts altogether (ibid.: 16, 19).

'retribution' must be considered means that aim to subtly 'control' prisoners who will subsequently re-enter society. Tactically, from a political perspective, this new disciplinary mechanism availed to implement relations of power as well as, incidentally, shape domains of knowledge (ibid.: 23, 28): by the by, discipline managed to sustain itself automatically and be ascertained as an effective substitute for uninterrupted surveillance in prison cells (not to forget outside societies at large).

Altogether, in a nutshell, prisons, rules, and regulations are designed to guard those in power, but not ordinary persons; otherwise stated, there is a distinction between the rights of superior and the rights of inferior segments of populaces as a result of a difference in power (Risi in ibid.: 47). So, prisons are not geared in the direction of 'all in the name of all', but for a very few, first and foremost (ibid.: 276); in which event, confinement is not employed to reduce misconduct (even if it may), but to deliver a productive labour force that fulfils all and any requisites of free-market industries. Nowadays, 'corrective' detention, rather than forced labour (as practiced before modernity), is what is needed since discipline increases and coordinates skills as well as efficacy (ibid.: 24f., 210). Simultaneously, it gives rise to 'a collection of separated individualities without feelings of solidarity, community, etc.' (ibid.: 177, 201).

Unquestionably, on the other hand, Foucault was aware some prisons genuinely sought to educate prisoners and re-integrate them into society: namely, the Walnut Street, Ghent, and Gloucester prisons (ibid.: 124). Nonetheless, he affirmed that real change could solely emerge by the act of fathoming fundamental motivations that underpin criminal actions (ibid.: 252): in this association, Foucault's own — admittedly, ideological — stance was criminality originates as a result of 'alienation' in society and, particularly, profound socio-economic divisions (ibid.: 276), which conclusively indicates there might be a bright side to what could be made of prisons if oppressive relations of power were resolved.

Foucault's unorthodox understanding of the role of prisons from the point of view of power — as opposed to rationality — is a matter more or less ignored in contemporary researches. Clearly, the actual role of education is mystified, whilst there is somehow an ideological undercurrent underneath Foucault's comprehensions; undoubtedly, at the same time, prisons are useful instruments for managing populations; in which event, of course, prison education becomes irrelevant in itself, but useful when it is designed to result in a better and more productive labour-force — obviously, from this viewpoint, whether humans have rights or anything, including education, would not really matter, apart from 'power' and 'control'.

Conclusion

Primarily, this paper's contribution to current academic literature is two-fold: it introduced Foucault's relations of 'power' and 'control' as an important yet neglected aspect of the nature of prisons and education in prisons; in addition, it re-visited Kantianism through Kant's critique of Utilitarianism, and its particular strength as a 'rational' theory in relation to prison education. Furthermore, the following assessments were agreed upon. Firstly, Utilitarianism offers the least convincing defence of prisoners' right to education, as it is based on 'experience' and is unable to offer an accurate estimate of what may be the best possible solution (either now or at a future date), while it does not see the value of what is our 'rational' faculty. Secondly, although Kantianism offers the most convincing formal defense of prisoners' right to education, it lacks clarity and unity in actual practice, particularly in relation to 'dignity' and 'autonomy'. Thirdly, Foucault's study of the origins and structural functions of prisons set the entire topic in a socio-political context and showcased how prisons may not have a benevolent intention in essence, and that 'power' is what ultimately determines one's personal rights; in a manner of speaking, Foucault's exposition showed that we must not be too focused on formal issues to the neglect of what may actually go on in the background. Otherwise, according to Fyodor Dostoevsky's (1821–1881) *Crime and Punishment*, we face nihilistic attitudes amidst individuals that stand for themselves and respect their own subjective points of view only. Optimistically, the sorts of functions that education can play in such societies would require other investigations henceforth.

BIBLIOGRAPHY

Beck, L. W. 1993. Translator's Introduction. In: I. Kant, *Critique of Practical Reason*. New Jersey: Prentice Hall, pp. vii-xix.

Coates, S. 2016. *Unlocking Potential: A review of education in prison.* [online]. Available at: https://assets.publishing.service.gov.uk/government/uploads/system/uploads/attachment_data/file/524013/education-review-report.pdf [Accessed 4 April 2020]

Critchley, S. 2001. *Continental Philosophy: A Very Short Introduction.* Oxford: Oxford University Press.

Darkenwald, G. G., & Merriam, S. B. 1982. *Adult Education: Foundations of Practice*. New York: Harper Collins Publishers.

Ellington, J. W. 1993. Introduction. In: I. Kant, *Grounding for the Metaphysics of Morals — with On a Supposed Right to Lie Because of Philanthropic Concerns*. Indianapolis: Hackett Publishing Company, pp. v-xiii.

Farley, H. & Pike, A. 2016. 'Engaging prisoners in education: Reducing risk and recidivism'. *Advancing Corrections: Journal of the International Corrections and Prisons Association* 1, pp. 65-73.

Foucault, M. 1991. *Discipline and Punish: The Birth of the Prison.* London: Penguin Books.

Gray, J. 1991. Introduction. In: J. S. Mill, *On Liberty and Other Essays*. Oxford: Oxford University Press, pp. vii-xxx.

Hamlyn, D. W. 1988. *A History of Western Philosophy*. London: Penguin Books.

Heywood, A. 1994. *Political Ideas and Concepts: An Introduction*. Hampshire: The Macmillan Press.

Kant, I. 1993a. *Critique of Practical Reason*. New Jersey: Prentice Hall.

Kant, I. 1993b. *Grounding for the Metaphysics of Morals — with On a Supposed Right to Lie Because of Philanthropic Concerns*. Indianapolis: Hackett Publishing Company.

Kant, I. 2018. *Critique of Pure Reason*. New York: Dover Publications.

Laub, J. H., Sampson, R. J. 2001. 'Understanding desistance from crime'. *Crime and Justice* 28, pp. 1-69.

Mill, J. S. 1991. *On Liberty and Other Essays*. Oxford: Oxford University Press.

Nagel, T. 2013. Foreword. In: R. Nozick, *Anarchy, State, and Utopia*. New York: Basic Books, pp. xi-xviii.

Nozick, R. 2013. *Anarchy, State, and Utopia*. New York: Basic Books.

Russel, B. 1947. *History of Western Philosophy and its Connection with Political and Social Circumstances from the Earliest Times to the*

Present Day. London: George Allen and Unwin.

Vorhaus, J. 2014. 'Prisoners' right to education: A philosophical survey'. *London Review of Education* 12 (2), pp. 162-174.

Warr, J. no date. *Boxed in? Applying to University with a Criminal Record*. [online]. Available at: https://moodle.ucl.ac.uk/mod/resource/view.php?id=1632867 [Accessed 3 April 2020]

SECTION II

ON SOPHIE, JEAN-JACQUES ROUSSEAU, AND WOMEN'S EDUCATION

INITIAL THOUGHTS

> People often criticize my films for being pessimistic; there are certainly many reasons for being pessimistic but I don't see my films that way. They're founded in the belief that revolution doesn't belong on the cinema screen but outside in the world. Never mind if a film ends pessimistically but exposes certain mechanisms clearly enough to show people how they work and the ultimate effect is not pessimistic. My goal is to reveal such mechanisms in a way that makes people realize the necessity of changing their own reality.
> — *Rainer Werner Fassbinder, Catalyst for the New German Cinema Movement*

It may be necessary to remind the reader that Jean-Jacques Rousseau (1712–78) has had no less influence on 'progressive education' than John Dewey (1859–1952) in the 20th century. Manifestly, something confirmed by John Darling (1994: 16) in his opinion that subsequent literature upon this movement were mere 'footnotes' to a seminal work, which Rousseau titled *Emile, or On Education*. Revealingly, a work of philosophical fiction was published in the year of 1762 within the Republic of Geneva and France, even though the author additionally completed a second and more full discussion on politics, headed *The Social Contract*, in the same year. Yet, with censures increasingly received, Rousseau found both works not only far exceeded the patience of 'the powers that be', but its consequences required a rather unhesitant eviction from his hometown than at that time he had any leisure to grant upon it. Effectively, he was hunted and thrown out of the Continent by deeply-suspect officialdoms. Reputedly, other proceedings led to the public burning of his books.

By the end of the year, this had produced on his part a pressing application to visit England, and indeed when he met David Hume (1711–1776) to live therein for a few years. However, a different plan appeared more prudential to his health and safety when his sentiments towards Hume turned away into another direction: apparently, the reason his sentiments had grown into a greater suspicion was assigned to that Scottish gentleman's (unfounded) plot to poison and kill Rousseau. Anxiously, therefore, he left England for France, never to return. All the same, with some earnestness, one may be given several reasons to imagine, that his impact on the proceedings of the French Revolution were of no little consequence, but instead reckoned to communicate a beacon of light that proved effective in transmitting national liberty and equality to any description of peoples.

Either way, there should be no mistake *Emile*'s received influence on the 'constitution' of educational practices and pedagogies is not insubstantial. All in all, those who cultivate the view that *Emile* solely reveals practices that aim to maintain genuine principles of education, will take good care to deliberate how that author's politics, philosophy, and religion shaped his overall bodies of thought. Simultaneously, *Emile* seems to have generated much negative opinion from reputable pundits. The most significant relates to the final chapter, named 'Sophie' (or 'Sophy' in some translations), which is about women's education. Sophie is also the protagonist's (Emile) future wife or female counterpart.

In the main, the chief criticism of 'Sophie' arises from differences in the manner in which, Rousseau claims, Sophie's character (as a woman) should be educated. For example, Rousseau suggests that Emile's bride-to-be should be taught things that traditionally occupy an exclusively female sphere, such as knitting, playing with dolls, child-rearing, and housekeeping. Yet, on the other hand, Emile is given the liberty to travel, explore and go on adventures without any apparent constriction. Essentially, he is not confined to the four walls of the house. It is this sense of inequality between the chapter on Sophie and the rest of the book (four other chapters) that has earned the severest of criticisms from the likes of early or proto-feminists, such as Mary Wollstonecraft (1759–1797), author of *A Vindication of the Rights of Woman*, and others more recently.

That being said, the contention of this section is that Rousseau's apprehension regarding women's education has been misunderstood and, therefore, necessarily requires clarification. To that end, it is divided into four chapters. The first outlines Rousseau's general thoughts outside the sphere of education, including politics, philosophy, and religion, as shown in his other major works, *The Social Contract*, *Discourses on Inequality*, *Discourses on Arts and Sciences*, *The Confessions*, and *The Reveries of the Solitary Walker*. The second chapter, subsequently, expounds his understanding of education as described in the first four chapters in *Emile*, which are purely about Emile's education and Rousseau's view on pedagogy; tensions are sought and examined, in turn. The third chapter, afterward, extrapolates Sophie's education according to Rousseau and sets out criticisms from the standpoints of a number of sources — past and contemporary. Lastly, the fourth chapter clarifies key misinterpretations of 'Sophie' by drawing on relevant contemporary studies on Rousseau and a reading of his wider work and life.

At this point, it is worth mentioning the primary methodology in Philosophy of Education is inherently qualitative. As such, since this applies to the subject framework of this thesis, there has been no use of quantitative data. Therefore, the primary sources employed for the purposes of this research constitute original sources by the relevant authors (including Rousseau, Mary Wollstonecraft, J. S. Mill, and Plato) as well as secondary sources in recent commentaries about Rousseau. Where appropriate, material from Rousseau's autobiography has been applied too to provide a wider interpretation.

All in all, the most significant conclusion of this dissertation is that 'Sophie' cannot be understood separately from the wider context of Rousseau's philosophy and politics. All meaning, the conclusions in the final chapter of this hypothesis must be viewed in this manner, even though Rousseau never claimed to have given us a perfect theory applicable to all circumstances or zeitgeist. Ultimately, by way of looking at original sources, my postulation endeavours to reinvigorate the work of a philosopher, whose corpus appears to have lost influence in a myriad of contemporary works, which seem to have forgotten that the pioneers of philosophy had offered potential solutions to today's questions on education centuries ago.

I. OF ROUSSEAU

> I found that dance, music, and literature is how I made sense of the world ... it pushed me to think of things bigger than life's daily routines ... to think beyond what is immediate or convenient.
> — *Mikhail Baryshnikov, Senior Ballerino*

Jean-Jacques Rousseau is not a man whose thoughts can be simplified in a brief passage, especially when his ideas ranged from such things as discourses on arts, sciences, inequality, languages, politics, philosophy, education, and spiritualism. It is sometimes also forgotten that he was a musician and composer. Be that as it may, whilst the focus of this thesis is on his understanding of women's education, this topic cannot be examined properly without being put in the context of Rousseau's broader worldview and core principles. This decision is made on the basis that Rousseau's work on education, as Jimack stressed, cannot be studied in isolation from his wider philosophical works as the two are 'interdependent and overlapping' (Jimack, 1983: 16, 10). As such, in two sections, this chapter examines, firstly, Rousseau's general understanding of progress, inequality, and human nature; and, secondly, his religious conviction and politics. Overall, this should provide an all-round view of Rousseau's philosophy before delving into his account of apposite education.

Part I: Progress, Inequality, and Human Nature

It is worth mentioning that whilst Rousseau consented to the impossibility of making decisive conclusions regarding human nature in its original state, he claimed his arguments were based on his observations. Either way, understanding human nature is important as it allows us to know what our natural rights are (Rousseau, no date: 7). In this respect, Rousseau was influenced by the works of social-contract theorists, such as Thomas Hobbes (1588–1679) and John Locke (1632–1704), who argued that the state of nature — or, in other words, 'the real or hypothetical condition of human beings before or without political association' — determined the limits or rights of political authority, and thereby rights of individuals, within human societies (Munro, 2020). For Hobbes, to illustrate, 'the state of nature is characterised by the "war of every man against every man," a constant and violent condition of competition in which each individual has a natural right to everything, regardless of the interests of others' (ibid.). Hobbes, thuswise, believed self-preservation was the *law* of nature or simply a human being's natural right. Locke, on the other hand, argued that one could maintain, by way of reason, 'that being all equal and independent, no one ought to harm another in his life, liberty, or possessions' — as their naturally endowed rights (ibid.).

Against this historical context, Rousseau's understanding of human nature was generally positive and optimistic. This was most evident in his famous idea that '[m]an [sic.] is born free and everywhere he is in chains' (Rousseau, 1968: 49); that humans are naturally good and virtuous, without any element of 'original sin', as propounded during the Age of Faith before him (for example, by the likes of Saint Augustine). Instead, he contended people were corrupted as a consequence of a number of important evils in society. Particularly, in his earlier works, he stated that arts, literature, and the sciences in society were corrupting influences on human conduct that stifled their sense of liberty, which they possessed in the state of nature, and deceptively led 'them to love their own slavery' — metaphorically speaking, like 'garlands of flowers' that are flung 'over their chains which weight them down' (Rousseau, 2008: 3). Essentially, 'noble savages' who lived in the state of nature lost their innocence when they started to form societies. Curiously, this is why Rousseau was often considered an outsider and abused as a traitor to the cause of the *philosophes* — namely, partisans of the Age of Reason, such as Diderot, who advocated progress in terms of development and organisation of empirical knowledge to improve life on earth — due to his open rejection of such Baconian notions of Enlightenment values (France, 1987: 5), and his argument that technological and intellectual advances had not enhanced the moral condition of humanity, but led to human vice and corruption.

To demonstrate his point, Rousseau compared Sparta to Athens: in the former, life revolved around public spirit, solidarity, and friendship, strengthened by simple arts; the latter life, on the other side, was contaminated by decadent arts and sciences. Metaphorically speaking, by simple arts, Rousseau meant practices that stayed true to honest human nature as he hypothesised it among 'noble savages', whereas decadent arts referred to practices that disguised the true constituents of humanity through superficial ornamentation (like oration, which Rousseau felt was designed for pure effect as opposed to developing one's virtuous behaviours). Be that as it may, for Rousseau, this was the crucial difference that led Athenians to their early downfall before Spartans. In fact, Rousseau modelled his understanding of Athens in terms of the effect of time and society, and what would be really left eventually: like the submerged statue of Glaucus which was 'so disfigured by time, seas and tempests, that it looked more like a wild beast than a god' (Rousseau, no date: 6). Analogously, this is why Rousseau respected such traditional values as simplicity, useful work, affection, family life, and piety which he also associated with his native Switzerland; for only such things lay closest to what he thought the most ideal state of existence: in the form of the 'noble savage' (the 'wild beast' of Glaucus after appearances fell).

So conjectured, although Rousseau was sceptical of the untrammelled embrace of arts and sciences, the publication of his second major text, *Discourses on Inequality*, demonstrated his view of inequality as another source for society's corruption prior to the advent of arts and sciences. For Rousseau, inequality, which was 'manifestly against the Law of Nature' to begin with (ibid.: 9), consisted of two kinds: one based on natural or physical inequalities established by nature, such as age and health; the other based on moral or political inequality, consisting of riches, position and such (ibid.). The latter was rather apprehended as artificial and incompatible with the natural person, solely because in the state of nature, all treated one another equally and inequality existed only in the sense of physical differences, and it could not be created voluntarily. In the state of nature, one could not sell oneself to another person even through one's own direct consent; or be exploited and made dependent on another (Rousseau, 1968: 69). This is because (foreshadowing Karl Marx, in some ways) the plight of the second inequality (moral or political) chiefly arose from private property as a by-product of the emergence of society and enclosure of land, through the cultivation of the earth, by some hierarchically-niched individuals. In this manner, through private ownership, people were born (by chance) into certain positions, rank and riches, wherein also were born senses of superiority and inferiority amidst persons — who, otherwise, would have treated one another equally despite physical inequalities. Private property, therefore, allowed inequality of talents and skills to result in inequality of material possessions, which led to the slavery of others as well as conflict when people's passions were excited (Cranston, 1968: 21); and as society bred war, there emerged a demand for law to ensure order and peace (ibid.): something particularly significant for the rich since any war threatened not only their possessions but their lives (ibid.).

Furthermore, it should be mentioned, Rousseau believed primitive humans had no moral relations with one another (Rousseau, no date: 18), in that they were pure and innocent (but 'atomised'; Parry, 2019: 75) persons existing apart from each other.

Although Rousseau does not explain how moral relations emerged, he mentioned a number of its key consequences. Speaking of sexual relations between human beings, Rousseau distinguished between the physical and moral ingredients, stating that the physical was the desire that urged a union between the sexes, while the moral was the fixation of desire upon one person only (ibid.: 21). Rousseau thought the latter was non-existent for the savage as their minds were simply incapable of comprehending abstract ideas of regularity, proportion, or beauty (ibid.). The savage, due to a lack of moral relations, was protected (so to speak) from violent fits of passion, which is why they were less subject to disputes or jealousies (ibid.). Therefore (as Aristotle similarly believed), savages gathered together either for the sake of pleasure or utility, that is fulfilling an instinctual need for reproduction, as opposed to anything that related to 'goodness' (virtue) for its own alleged rewards.

Another related aspect to the absence of moral relations in the state of nature is that savages did not calculate the consequences of their actions. So, if one stole something, it was out of desire, never out of deliberate design: especially because the former would have been merely peaceful and ignorant, whereas the latter harmful and wicked. This example somewhat relates to Rousseau's disagreement with Hobbes' statement that wickedness parallels a 'robust child', one that is at the same time strong but dependent, whilst demanding the fulfilment of its passions from others (ibid.: 19). According to Rousseau, Hobbes' statement was contradictory because a child cannot be strong (robust) but dependent at the same time. He or she is weak simply because it depends on its mother for nourishment; it becomes independent, more likely, when it grows enough to gain strength.[8] In this context, humans were strong and independent in the state of nature because there were no relations that made them dependent on others. The moral (not to mention physical) distance, in a way, ensured individuals did not need remedies or physicians because there were fewer causes of sickness in the state of nature

---

[8] Analogously, Rousseau noted animals become 'weaker, timid and servile' when they are domesticated and begin to depend on their owner (ibid.: 13).

compared to one of socialised living (ibid.: 12). All suggesting, a being whose heart and body was in health and at ease could not possibly suffer misery or act by design against the interests of other beings (including animals).

In this context, additionally, the 'noble savage' had no imagination nor did his or her heart make any demands (ibid.: 14): they had few wants, which were easily supplied, whilst they lacked the knowledge to want more; beings which were 'wholly wrapped up in the feeling of [their] present existence' (ibid.: 15). As an aside, this is relevant to the fact that in the state of nature, human beings were not able to recognise 'pride' or '*amour-propre*'. This meant they could not be inflicted by unhappiness for wanting the impossible or be induced to compare themselves with others in envy, admiration or overexertion of power. Crucially, '*amour-propre*' was an 'evil mutation' of 'self-love' or '*amour-de-soi*', which was an innocent sentiment found in the natural man (Cranston, 1968: 32), meaning that happiness could only be achieved by restricting one's desires to the attainable. While emotional self-sufficiency was the natural state of primitive men, suppression of natural inclinations was the proper state for the modern man. Obviously, conscience would play an important role in this matter because it would turn knowledge of what is good into the love of good (and goodness is lack of malice). According to Rousseau's convoluted and multi-levelled view of conscience, it is the only quality that elevates human beings above other animals, thereby making them 'godly' since it functions as an 'immortal and celestial voice' amid their attributes (see the following reference for further elaboration of this point; Kodelja, 2015: 198).

On that note, it should be pointed out, in the state of nature compassion is characterised by a being's sensibility to one's welfare and preservation, as well as simultaneously 'a natural repugnance at seeing any other sensible being […] suffer pain or death' (Rousseau, no date: 8). By implication, Rousseau stated, as compassion was less likely present in the state of reason, so generosity, clemency, friendship, and the like were more likely demonstrable in the state of nature. In this sense, another one of Rousseau's analogies states, a philosopher will put his hands on his ears to stop hearing a murder being committed below his window, whilst an uncivilised savage who obeys the promptings of its humanity will react immediately to save the other being from death (ibid.: 20). Hence, compassion not only moderated the violence of *self*-preservation (which cares only for itself), but it took the place of laws, virtues and morals to safeguard the survival of the whole species (ibid.: 20).[9]

That said, it is important to note that when mankind created society and began to incorporate morality into its system of thinking, it became unable to revert to its original state both physically and psychologically. An act of return to the state of nature, Rousseau asserted, would have simply led to disaster because the socialised person had already lost its innocence forever: 'without the culture he had denounced, modern man would be even more vicious than he is' (Rousseau cited in Jimack, 1983: 15). Hence, Rousseau's solution was that since socialised individuals could not do without society, humanity's quest was decidedly to evolve and strive toward an elevated form of society that ensured its peoples were 'virtuous'. 'Virtue' for Rousseau, above all, came from a sense of self-denial accompanied by devotion for the good of others. To be sure, although one might recognise that this ostensibly contradicts Rousseau's original emphasis on following one's natural propensities, Rousseau nevertheless justifies this point in terms of a 'higher' happiness in the long run. He believed, therewith, that individuals (even if born good) had to actively pursue 'virtue' through an effort of will. As the (historical) 'natural' person was a non-social and non-moral being, 'virtue' came only when the person received moral responsibility after forming relationships — whereby one overcame 'passions in the interest of others' (France, 1987: 10).

Ultimately, therefore, 'virtue' could only take place within a communal setting. For Rousseau, however, the formation of an ideal society was inevitably inseparable from politics and religion. The

---

[9] Certainly, since animals partake in this ruling too as sensible beings, Rousseau mentioned they do not deserve to be ill-treated by humankind (ibid.: 8); foreshadowing discussions on animal rights!

next section delves into these two topics, outlining the other half of Rousseau's theoretical framework.

Part II: Religion and Politics

As it happens, Rousseau's religious beliefs shared especial similarities with the standard eighteenth-century deism ('Unitarian or Socinian' according to Maurice), represented for example by Voltaire, Locke, or Malebranche (Jimack, 1983: 39; Cranston, 1968: 39). In short, while Rousseau believed in the existence of God, he expressed serious reservations about the Church. Furthermore, he was diametrically opposed to the Christian idea of original sin or, indeed, the fall of humanity. As some type of deist, therefore, he reasoned individuals to be capable of knowing — through their own logic and conscience — religious and moral truths. Hence, he opposed intermediaries, in the form of the Church, between himself and the truth. Rousseau's religion, in short, was his acceptance of things that are demonstrable to reason (as a kind of critical filter) and rejection of all that are not. Faith, in other words, did not play any role in Rousseau's religion; and while he ardently supported toleration as a core principle, he rejected intolerance per se. One has to remember this was in the intolerant environment of Louis XV (1715–74) France, which had outlawed Protestantism, demonstrating the genuine radicalism of Rousseau during this period. Lastly, it is interesting that while Rousseau was opposed to the Church, he was far more sympathetic to Christians than certain other *philosophes* who appeared to condone 'atheistic' values (Jimack, 1983: 42).

Either way, Rousseau's spiritual position is perhaps explained by the following sentence: 'I love to contemplate Him in His works while my heart uplifts itself to Him' (Rousseau, 1953: 225). The central idea in this respect is that God's existence may be inferred from all creations in nature. Part of this suggestion arises from the fact Rousseau regularly withdrew from towns to live in the idyllic countryside — not unlike Emile and his tutor as outlined in the next chapter (Jimack, 1983: 25). For him, this somewhat resembled the ideal periods of tribal life (as outlined previously) when savages were much closer to nature. Of course, this also meant Rousseau was able to convey the significance of feelings over the brain in terms of the apprehension of truth and let loose his imagination (Cohen, 1953: 10); 'I felt before I thought' (Rousseau, 1953: 19). The entirety of his *Reveries of the Solitary Walker*, as a matter of course, is a practice to delineate a closer, inward relationship with God as a solitary being (Parry, 2011: 21).

But, what is noteworthy, Rousseau believed this was different from religion as a citizen, corresponding to which one followed the religion established by one's country or 'general will' (Rousseau, 1968: 181), comprising unique dogmas, rituals as well as external forms of worship — that is, instead of an individual's own devotion to God as the simple religion of the Gospel. Rousseau noted, noteworthily, that state religion is more important than private religion and must be supreme (Cranston, 1968: 40). In broad terms, this explains why Rousseau so easily converted to Catholicism from Protestantism after his departure from Geneva (the city of Calvinism: a denomination within the Protestant movement), but eventually returned to the latter fold when he resumed his citizenship once more later in his life.

With that in mind, the significance of citizenship is relevant in other terms as well, in particular, relating to the duty to one's native country. Briefly, while Rousseau admitted there were no ideal societies or governments in reality, people owe something to the country they dwell in, and that they should, as model citizens, pay this back. This would allow individuals to attain moral liberty ('virtue' as defined above) as opposed to physical liberty found within the state of nature. In turn, existing societal corruptions would be overcome and harmony attained by way of realising one's true nature. In this connection, interestingly, *Emile* was part of Rousseau's guidepost regarding how education could bring about an individual's 'natural' state against the pressures of society and the powers of the state. Although the term *nature* may be interpreted in differing ways — sometimes in the historical sense, as in before society, or, indeed, in the psychological sense, as in primitive people's dispositions, or, most often, in either sense — for Rousseau, one's 'natural' state was synonymous with 'virtuosity' as an elevated quality (Jimack, 1983: 18f.).

Although there are important debates about the conflict between Rousseau's love of nature and enthusiasm for society — in other words, between individualism and self-less devotion to the state as a citizen — he believed the two were not only compatible, but complemented each other. Ultimately, this is because all members of society unreservedly had to submit to what Rousseau called the 'general will' ('*volonté générale*') enshrined within a 'social contract'. When materialised, the 'general will' would embody people's 'real interests' or will as a single entity (Jimack, 1983: 21). In this form of society, every citizen is a legislator (Cranston, 1968: 20). Only administration in government would be conducted by a select few who specialise in dedicated roles — in order to execute the law (ibid.: 30). From this point of view, as the nature of a nation's government determined its actions and whatever was done by it (ibid.: 13), the ideal society, for Rousseau (as a Republican thinker and antagonist towards any notion of a 'divine right of kings'), comprised continuous political participation by its citizens.

His, therein, was a radical form of democracy, one in which ultimate authority rested not in mere representatives, but in people as one whole. As an aside, Rousseau's political beliefs were based on a form of primitive democracy that he had observed in Swiss cantons, which were politically sovereign societies, the small size of which meant they could meet regularly to legislate and decide on state-matters as citizens (ibid.: 19). Obviously, as the Swiss cantons were very similar to the democracy of the ancient Greek city-states, there have been a number of criticisms, namely one by an ancient Roman historian, Tacitus, who saw them as a type of Alemannic democracy, stating that they were tribal and barbaric, and capable of functioning merely in a simple form of culture and a small, face-to-face society wherein everyone knew one another and considered them as more or less equal (ibid.).

Said so, it is of note that, while individual acquiescence to agreed laws is acceptable, mere compliance to another individual's arbitrary decision-making should be prohibited, in Rousseau's mind — liberty, in essence, demands that one must not be subjected to the will of another person, no matter how well-placed, but only to the dictates of the 'general will' as elaborated below (ibid.: 32). Obviously, this is in direct contrast to Hobbes' belief in absolute sovereignty, one in which people are either ruled or are free, as the two could not operate in conjunction (ibid.: 27). Rousseau, instead, argued the fullest freedom was possible in a civil society only, because freedom and 'virtue' were inseparable from one another (ibid.: 28). Therefore, his solution to Hobbes' problem was that human beings could be ruled and be free at the same time only if they ruled themselves by way of actively partaking in the 'general will' — that is to say, in law-making (ibid.: 29-30). This is in view of the fact people would not voluntarily 'chain' themselves if they were sovereign and subject at the same time — unless they were ignorant and did so unwittingly (ibid.: 37). (Certainly, needless to reiterate, neither could the rich buy another human being, or the poor be forced to sell themselves; Rousseau, 1968: 96.)

Here, it is important to differentiate between the 'will of all' and the 'general will' as the two are quite separate. Briefly, the former is an 'empirical concept' in that the 'will' is what all will; the latter is a 'normative concept' in that 'its connexion with right is a matter of definition' (Cranston, 1968: 37). Put simply, the 'general will' consists of the *common* interest as a whole, while the 'will of all' consists of studying *individual* (private) interests independently from the collective and is no more than the sum of individual thoughts put together. The 'general will', at the end of the day, is what remains after the plus and minus of individual wills cancel each other out (Rousseau, 1968: 72). The 'social pact' essentially includes everything that is indispensable to each person included. Put differently, as Maurice stated, 'it is the majority *interpretation* of the general will which is binding and not the majority *will*' (emphasis added; Cranston, 1968: 38). The outcome is a public person united in its ego, life, and will with the 'general will' (Rousseau, 1968: 61): namely, they become citizens of a 'body politic' (ibid.).

In practice, this means as everybody subscribes to the 'social contract', in the first place, they have to accept the decision of the majority in the formulation of the law when speaking of the 'general will'. In which instance, the minority might have to accept the 'general will' by force (Cranston, 1968: 38). According to Rousseau, however, such instances are rare and more like anomalies. Therefore, those individuals would need to be punished because they are disobeying the law. As such, when Rousseau speaks of a person who may need to be forced to be free, he is not speaking of whole communities but the occasional individual who, due to his passions, may disobey the voice of the 'general will' within him (ibid.: 35). By penalising a law-breaker, consequently, society is teaching a lesson for which an offender would be grateful eventually (ibid.).

Be that as it might, Rousseau also contended that laws today did not reflect what they were supposed to in society — in accordance with the 'general will'. Rather, existing laws reflected the interests of the powerful or the stronger against those of the weaker (ibid.: 37). It is for this reason, he claimed, there were two types of law, in general: 'actual law', which is law as it is in the world; and 'true law', which is how it should be, that is, according to the requirements of 'natural law' as mentioned above (ibid.). Briefly, the former aimed to maintain order, even though it was eventually detrimental and was the source of crimes and disorders (Rousseau, 1953: 306); the latter aimed to maintain justice and public welfare. Put differently, in a Rousseauian society, 'rights based on might' (order for the benefit of the rich and powerful) are replaced by 'rights based on law' (in accordance with the 'general will' for the benefit of all) (Cranston, 1968: 33). In this context, it is worth mentioning, despite the impression Rousseau gives regarding the absoluteness of the 'general will', it can never be unlimited since it is constrained by 'natural law', which governs the world (ibid.: 38). And 'natural law' is significant for Rousseau because of his belief in religion and piety; something perhaps demonstrated by the fact he thought there were three other authorities higher than the state: God, natural law, and honour (ibid.).

Conclusion

All in all, it may be said there are two great themes that run throughout Rousseau's complex works: 'virtue' and 'liberty'. Even then, Rousseau's ideas are often rejected as far too optimistic, if not highly abstract and theoretical. Nevertheless, as he himself admitted, his ideas were based purely on his personal experiences, his hometown Geneva, readings regarding anthropological accounts at the time of newly discovered peoples around the globe, not to mention ancient Greek and Roman literature. Contrarily, these two themes have their origin, as previously observed, in Rousseau's unexpectedly religious thought. Without religion, in the broadest sense of the word, neither could 'virtue' nor 'liberty' be attained by any person; for devotion to state religion ensures virtue, and devotion to inward religion ensures liberty (by way of connecting with Nature). When both are attained, we have a model citizen who is in complete harmony with other citizens as well as Nature beyond the 'general will'. Rousseau, thence, never advocates a return to the original state of the 'noble savage', but rather transcendence to a selfless, virtuous being. Now that we are familiar with Rousseau's broader theories, it is time to turn to his views on how this could be achieved through Emile's education.

II. ON EMILE

> The heart of the Waldorf method is that education is an art — it must speak to the child's experience. To educate the whole child, his heart and his will must be reached, as well as the mind.
> — *Rudolf Steiner, Author and Founder of Anthroposophy*

As his favoured book, none other had more influence on Rousseau's life than *Emile, or On Education*. Published in the same year (1762) as *The Social Contract*, it gained so much attention it caused a seismic shift in Rousseau's peaceful, idealised life within the rural French landscapes. Indeed, on the hunt by various authorities in the Continent, he was forced into exile in England. In any event, this was not engendered by the misleading subtitle of the book. Particularly, apart from education, *Emile* also made dangerous assertions about such emotive subjects as radical politics and religion, while almost certainly the 'Profession of Faith of the Savoyard Vicar', in Book IV, led to his volume being banned in Geneva, since it was read as a rejection of orthodox Christianity — perhaps, tangentially, this is why he called it a 'treatise on the original goodness of man [sic.] in *all* his aspects (Rousseau in France, 1987: 13). All the same, *Emile* is divided into five chapters and, as a 'half treatise half novel' (Jimack, 1974: vii), follows the education of a boy called Emile from his infancy to adulthood and the education of a girl called Sophie (in the last chapter) as Emile's counterpart and future wife. The chapter on Sophie, specifically, revolves around the application of the same principles (discussed in the rest of the book) on women's education.

So outlined, this chapter aims to examine, solely, Rousseau's understanding of education in its general sense. Therefore, here we are concerned only with Emile's education, before Sophie's is discussed in depth in the next chapter. To that end, the first part broadly draws together the personal development of Emile's education, in terms of his intellect and ability to understand reason. The second part, afterwards, sketches the social aspect of his education, in terms of his ability to socialise and form a family.

Before anything else, it must be mentioned, although Rousseau abandoned his children (against their mother's wishes), and many may question whether this behaviour indicates he was capable of arguing for any type of education, it is important to bear in mind his personal life and emotional idiosyncrasies, discussed in his autobiography, *Confessions*, to know that there were some acceptable reasons — particularly, an issue relating to his wife's family and her mother — which forced Rousseau to leave the lives of his five children to a foundlings' home (Kessen, 1978: 155). Either way, we are not to neglect the fact that Rousseau was already an experienced tutor of several children before he wrote *Emile*.

Part I: Personal Development

Although Rousseau wrote *Emile* with a general view of all children's education, he believed there were some exceptions to the rules he had set out in the book. Indeed, as attested in his *Confessions*, he believed his youth was rather different from that of other children, including Emile, as he claims he was more like a man than a child; that he was sufficiently mature to discuss complex subjects like religion — unlike other children (Rousseau, 1953: 67). Tellingly, he perceived himself as unusual, even though he thought such things as child prodigies were not common in reality and could not be trusted in most children as genuine. If asked how this was possible in his case, however, he would have probably drawn attention to *Robinson Crusoe* (his favourite novel), in which Crusoe, as the protagonist, was the first to explore a desolate island and learn to survive on his own without any assistance. Later, when Crusoe forms a friendship with a young indigenous man, who becomes his loyal personal assistant and student, Crusoe (like Rousseau) effectively becomes a self-taught 'pathfinder' as well as a tutor. As this was rare, Rousseau advocated that most children needed to be taught by another person according to the principles described in *Emile*.

To further contextualise, although *Emile* was not a pioneering work, specifically in terms of practical suggestions made about children's (particularly infants) upbringing and education — amongst those that came before Rousseau during the Age of Reason, for instance, Locke — it nevertheless introduced an original conception about education as a holistic process, instead of explicit pedagogical implications suggested beforehand. In this regard, for Rousseau, the development of a person's intellect and ability to make moral decisions may be described in successive stages, starting with the recognition of sensations as a baby to '*raison sensitive*', which is comparing sensations. This is, then, followed by the formation of '*ideas simples*' to the more fully-fledged reason, known as '*ideas complexes*' (Jimack, 1983: 59). Thereby, as Jimack suggested, Emile's education was an 'organically structured whole', whereby each phase was designed to suit a child's precise stage of development (ibid.: 74).

To be particular, the first stage in *Emile* (in the first two books) is up to the age of 12, called 'the Age of Nature', and primarily revolves around Emile's physical being in order to allow for its natural development as well as build a strong constitution in preparation for his intellectual and moral growth later in life. Emile's 'museum', as such, is the whole world (Rousseau, 1974: 375). Therefore, in keeping with Plato's *Republic*, which Rousseau had evidently read, the initial importance given to the physical body was because of the belief that without a strong constitution, one could not hope to develop the mind. To start with, this is why Rousseau advised against such things like swaddling or being prevented from exercising that attempted to ingrain discipline in children but, in fact, restrained their natural growth. From this standpoint, in another example, he also rejected the use of medicine to treat illnesses, due to their artificial nature and preventing a child from strengthening their natural immunity.

Essentially, Rousseau thought children had to be treated as they were — and not as adults — in the sense of a self-contained stage in development, a phase with its own characteristics and perfections. For Rousseau, children's happiness in the present rather than the future was important, particularly in view of the fact that at the time, many children died before they reached the age of seven. In this manner of speaking, as Rousseau strongly believed, happiness resembled in a sense the idyllic innocence of the 'noble savage', it should never have been taken away from children, and they deserved to be at the centre of a loving environment (Jimack, 1983: 50). This is why he disliked any type of traditional instruction, including the use of punishment, for he was adamant that children simply were not at a stage to understand the difference between right and wrong. He believed that children could only learn when they were curious to learn something and should never be forced to do so. In this phase of Emile's education, then, he will have no instructive lessons (say, in heraldry, ancient history, scripture, geography, or Latin) and will not even read books or learn anything by heart. Indeed, the child must not be forced to build the same habits as a previous day in order to 'leave the germ of his character free to show itself' (Rousseau in Jimack, 1974: xviii).

In this connection, not unlike Locke, Rousseau was influenced by 'sensationalism': that is to say, a form of 'empiricism' that saw experience as a source of knowledge, which convinced him that an education system that emphasised actual experience was more important than readings within the enclosed walls of a building. Put simply, only raw experience (or data) acquired by means of stimulating the five senses could allow one to begin to form simple or complex ideas or knowledge: 'Climates, seasons, sounds, colours, darkness, light, the elements, food, noise, silence, movement, repose: they all act on our machines, and consequences upon our souls' (Rousseau, 1953: 381). This early period, resultingly, is more of a 'negative' education (in other words, 'passive' learning instead of 'active' learning, as touched upon later), whereby the world is initially a textbook in itself (Jimack, 1983: 50), which is why explanation in words — rather than actions — must only be a last resort (ibid.: 63). The essential idea for Rousseau, herein, was that Emile would build a mass of 'raw material' from his five senses, which would be used for his future development after the completion of the first phase of his education. The entirety of 'the Age of Nature', therefore, would have to be dedicated to heightening and exploring each of Emile's five senses individually; never attempting to combine any together until the appropriate time.

Assuredly, regarding the next phase, whilst Rousseau believed in 'sensationalism', he did not adhere to the variations of such authors as Locke, who argued that experience was the be-all and end-all of knowledge — or mind as a *tabula rasa* ('blank slate'). By contrast, he argued judgments in mind were made by individuals through connections that they actively formed following the assimilation of experience from the senses. As it happens, Rousseau believed that language played an important part in this process by bridging the gap between 'pure sensation and the most simple knowledge' (Rousseau, no date: 15). Noticeably, also, Rousseau valued the utility of language in communicating ideas and facilitating the operation of human progress, as well as the prolonged period that this must have taken to reach its first mention (ibid.). As a matter of course, parenthetically, he suggested language initially originated in the intercourse between parents and children (ibid.: 16), while the first step was probably 'the simple cry of nature', followed subsequently by 'the inflections of the voice, and added gestures' (ibid.). Eventually, of course, language reached a stage when thoughts could be given constant form and perfect expression (ibid.: 17). Judgments, thus, were higher in quality than mere sense experience because they were formed by language, something which was learned from the moment of a child's birth.

In any event, he referred to such connections, specifically, in terms of '*ideas simples*' and '*ideas complexes*', as cited a little earlier. This entailed that after the first stage of his development, Emile must start to combine his senses (as well as continue to strengthen each) by way of exercising his reason (which leads to language); that is, in the sense of 'positive' education, or in other words the constructive learning process, from the age of twelve to fifteen as found in Book III. To illustrate, the case of a stick in water appearing bent showcases how Emile may train his comprehension (judgment) of the world by starting to form simple connections between raw 'data' realised from his senses (Jimack, 1983: 60). Taken together, in his account of education in astronomy, Emile would learn more about this subject by looking at the stars using self-made instruments, than if he spent a day reading books. Partly, this is still due to the fact the tutor has to be realistic about what is, or what is not, within the student's intellectual grasp. The tutor must take time to ensure genuine understanding rather than accelerating the pace of learning of the student at all times in this phase.

It is worth stressing, throughout this process, Emile must be kept under some form of authority, not only to control what things he comes into contact with, but also to effectively manage any behaviour issues in the process. Consequently, Rousseau believed part of his pedagogical practice involved methods that made Emile feel free, even though he lacked total freedom. This is perhaps most evident in Book III, in which Emile's progress is by 'ingeniously guided discovery' (Jimack, 1974: xvi). With this in view, although Rousseau may be hailed as a children's 'liberator' (Jimack, 1983: 46), reservations about the level of manipulation undertaken by the tutor during this educative process continues to raise concerns about the tutee's freedom. For Rousseau, part of the solution is that a person will feel free when something that is within reach is exclusively desired; in this sense, the tutor must be able to limit Emile's imagination to the achievable. Admittedly, that detailed, it is difficult to imagine total freedom in every other circumstance, for even primitive humans, as Rousseau observed, have certain restrictions on their freedom that cannot be overcome.

Above all, contrariwise, as the final objective of *Emile* is to attain one's 'natural' state or 'virtue' as a model citizen (and not to be corrupted by the chains of society), it is crucial that the tutor must be able to teach anything that is necessary for that purpose to the child. Interestingly, that is, by keeping Emile dependent on the tutor, Rousseau believed, the latter could teach the student dependence on the state or the 'Lawgiver', as a virtuous citizen (Cranston, 1968: 42) — even though he was against dependence on another person. Phrased differently, he stated that this was acceptable since this type of dependence was not too great to be excessive because it precluded dependence on all other people (as detailed in a prior section). The image of the 'Lawgiver' is clearly that of Emile's tutor (ibid: 42f.), in which case, the path to liberty would be voluntary submission to a benevolent tutor as opposed to having a master (ibid.: 43). All in all, it must be kept in mind that Rousseau does not advocate total freedom (as attempted, for instance, in A. S. Neill's Summerhill School), but an education system that directs a child's learning according to their interests, as observed by the tutor. This education system is free to the extent that it respects a student's needs and desires and never attempts to enforce authority directly; for Rousseau, children had to be inspired to learn, but never be forced — their lessons should never be gloomy or tiresome (Rousseau, 1974: 341).

In any event, apart from his intellectual growth, Emile is now (age 12 to 15) additionally ready to commence his learning a trade as part of his preparation to enter into the social phase of development (ibid.: 128ff.). In this respect, a trade might constitute things like watchmaking, carpentry, or other such crafts that allowed one to earn a living and provide basic necessities for one's future family. Certainly, for Rousseau, knowing a trade was also a characteristic of a model citizen (based on his observations of the Swiss cantons), that allowed one to contribute to society as well as achieve self-sufficiency, both of which would guarantee Emile's long-term happiness as a social and as a natural man. Noteworthily, to facilitate this process, Rousseau also claimed that Emile must read his favourite novel, *Robinson Crusoe* (by Daniel Defoe), as an appropriate thought experiment regarding a protagonist who is stranded on an island following a tempest at sea. Although, there are a number of overarching themes throughout the entire story, that of Crusoe's ability as a 'noble' savage to survive in a desolate island — and mature from a reckless boy not understanding the consequences of his actions to a man of experience — corresponds with Rousseau's idea of Emile's growth as a young man.

Further, it is at this stage that Emile is ready to begin his education in moral and religious matters. Following everything, Emile could not be taught any moral or religious lessons at a younger age; for he lacked sufficient experience to appropriately understand the complex meaning of religious or moral ideas, which could result in gross misunderstandings and the commitment of disastrous ethical breaches; what is more, his vocabulary could not outstrip his thoughts (Jimack, 1983: 60). Of course, the type of religion and morality taught is not unlike the religion outlined in the first chapter: whereby Emile must learn that God is an all-powerful, intelligent and benevolent creator, although He cannot be studied in any detail or comprehended.

Either way, having examined the implications of Rousseau's system of education on Emile's personal development, it is now time to delve into the phase in which Emile begins to learn about society and interacts with the world.

Part II: Social Development

While Emile's personal development is carried out in the idyllic countryside away from people in towns, his social development demands that Emile returns to society. Nonetheless, the reason Emile had to be taken away from the town he was born in, first and foremost, actually relates to Rousseau's classic assertion that the natural man is born good, but is corrupted by society. By being brought up away from people, principally, the tutor is protecting Emile from the corrupting influences of society. When the proper time arrives, however, it is important that the tutor introduces Emile to cities and people.

As it ensues, this stage in Emile's education and development usually coincides with his sexual awakening after the age of fifteen. Indeed, with the awakening of Emile's passions begins his socialising process and emotional growth since he develops pity, love, and friendship for fellow human beings. In other words, this stage prepares him to integrate into society and develop his moral intuition as part of this process. In a way, Rousseau wants to ensure Emile is able to make moral decisions for himself when he interacts with other people. Otherwise, he notes, Emile would be forced to bow to another's authority and, therewith, lose his freedom (ibid.: 64). For that reason, although he is now interacting with others, he continues to possess the freedom illustrated in the earlier books.

Relevantly, part of Emile's education involves studying poetry and languages, for these subjects will not only provide him with pleasure, but they will also be useful to him in the future by cultivating Emile's aesthetic taste to rely on his own inner resources: 'My main object in teaching him to feel and love beauty of every kind is to fix his affections and his taste on these, to prevent the corruption of his natural appetites' (Rousseau in Jimack, 1974: xvii). This is important at this stage of Emile's education to prevent the corruptions of society as he travels and sees people, at the same time as advancing towards self-sufficiency. To this end, Emile must likewise learn history and study what is instructive morally speaking in order to understand the true nature of humankind as part of his preparation to enter society. This is to ensure that, while Emile studies society and its various aspects, he always remains above it as a spectator.

When, thereafter, Emile has learned to think for himself and has been protected from prejudice and error, he is then ready to return to society. In this regard, Emile is taken around the world to observe people from all walks of life. This is important because a learned Emile must be aware of oppressive as well as oppressed parts of society. Of course, this reflects Rousseau's own experiences with the different classes — from the aristocratic families that he mingled with, to being an apprentice who at times stole fruits or other objects. In this respect, Rousseau wanted Emile to realise that the rich not only oppressed and despised the poor but contributed nothing to their own community in return (Jimack, 1983: 23); that they misused their riches, power, and influence (ibid.: 25); thoughts, fundamentally, reflected in his *Discourses on Inequality* (examined in the chapter preceding). At this juncture, reading economics and history books is the additional step Emile needs to take in order to learn more about human society and appreciate its moral aspects. At the same time, needless to say, Emile must not stop engaging in such things as hunting or other activities in nature that develop his senses.

All in all, Emile's socialising process has two integral outcomes. Foremost, the tutor must prevent Emile from exploring his sexuality, from the age of fifteen to twenty, as enumerated in Book IV, in order to ensure he is not corrupted by society. This is because sexuality, by nature, involves interaction with other people. In this fashion, since Emile is taken away from Sophie, the moment he starts to fall in love with her, there seems to be an element of 'safe distancing' in his learning. Secondly, in a related manner, the tutor's attempt to control and suppress Emile's natural or passionate feelings will develop his 'virtue' as a model citizen. In line with his belief in self-denial, Rousseau claimed that the subjugation of passions (especially sexual) was important to develop Emile's 'virtuous' nature. In essence, the tutor's aim by withdrawing Emile from Sophie is to channel his sexuality into love and marriage, in order to constitute a state of long-term happiness, as opposed to short-lived or infrequent gratification of intense (sexual) pleasures (ibid.: 76). All meaning, Emile must now leave Sophie partly to be worthy of her when he returns, so that Sophie may become the prize of his fidelity (Rousseau, 1974: 412). Certainly, Emile's lessons in socialisation will naturally lead not only to the love of his fellow citizens, but his own family as well.

The last stage in Emile's education is called 'the Age of Wisdom' (from twenty to twenty-five). It is at this stage that Emile is ready to learn religion and remember to reject the authority of the Church and discover truths for himself — replacing Christian revelation with human judgment (Jimack, 1974: xxi-xxii). Furthermore, to be worthy of Sophie, Emile's last stage of development also concerns his full knowledge of government, public morality, and political philosophy (Rousseau, 1974: 421). The obvious aim here is to prepare Emile to become a model citizen, ready to meet his society's demands. Emile, at the same time, must fully learn the value of freedom and lack of prejudice, as a condition that needs to be fulfilled before Sophie decides to marry him of her own will (ibid.: 436). When the above is realised, the end is characterised by the start of Emile's idyllic picture of his life with Sophie in the countryside. This is called 'the Age of Happiness'.

Having said that, what is noteworthy is that happiness with Sophie is not manifestly permanent. In fact, this idea is set out in Rousseau's unfinished sequel to *Emile*, titled *Emile and Sophie, or the Solitaries*, which discloses a somewhat unexpected future for Emile, in which Sophie is unfaithful to him (even though it is not clear if it were intended) and he finds himself in a distressful situation. Nevertheless, at this point, Emile begins to remember his tutor's last lesson on freedom as well as happiness, and concludes that notwithstanding what he has lost, he still has his life, reason, health, knowledge, talents, and virtue (not to mention admiration and ecstasies of nature) all of which inherently result in his view of happiness (Cohen, 1953: 13). In this manner, Emile uses his wisdom to regain self-control and vision of his destiny (Jimack, 1974: xii-xiii). In a sense, it may be argued Rousseau's support for living alone was partly connected with his own experience as a man, as noted in his *Reveries of the Solitary Walker*, when rejected by his fellow men and the love of his life (Mme de Warens), he sought to find the kind of self-sufficiency of emotional detachment he had preached in *Emile* (Rousseau, 1992: 13).

Conclusion

Generally speaking, there are certain significant problems with Rousseau's model of education. Perhaps the most obvious of all is that, ultimately, Emile's education is aristocratic in nature and maybe literally impossible to follow precisely and step-by-step, simply due to the sheer number of children, not to mention the insufficient number of private tutors. What is worse, Rousseau propounded that the tutor should be required to teach without payment, which in itself might drain a financially unstable tutor's professional motivation (particularly in current market-driven cultures). Furthermore, another contradistinction in terms of Rousseau's overall theorisation is illustrated by the fact that Emile's highly-structured socialising process is suddenly understood to be partial in praxis after he is absorbed into the life of a *secluded* family amid the countryside (following his marriage with Sophie). This is a de facto withdrawal from society, to be sure, because Emile is no longer engaged in the different cultural and political circles of the earlier phases. More precisely, any type of familial self-sufficiency psychologically removes Emile from the towns and other villages of his society, which is inconsistent with Rousseau's objectified ideal of a citizen embodying the life of the 'general will' (Jimack, 1983: 73).

Just the same, apart from practical problems and tensions within the theory, the core characteristics of Rousseau's type of education are still worth discussing. To summarise, Emile's education revolves around a unified theory that aims to promote happiness as the end goal, all through physical, intellectual, emotional, social, and spiritual development. For Rousseau, children's education must be undertaken in stages, broadly beginning from Emile's inward capabilities to his social skills. The entirety of these stages must incorporate the natural development of each child from a holistic point of view, so that their progression is never forced, but remains natural. In this way, unsurprisingly, Rousseau's subordination of details to the overall conception of learning was perhaps the most significant of his contributions to the field of education; an aspect that clearly distinguished his work from a writer such as Locke and eventually had a major influence on 'progressive education' in the last century. In some ways, although *Emile* continues to have an impact on modern debates around educational praxis, his viewpoints on feminine education have little support within the field. Having studied Emile's tuition, as a male tutee in this chapter, we will delve into Rousseau's view on the education of women.

III. CRITIQUING SOPHIE'S EDUCATION

> Children are encouraged to find their own learning situations in child-initiated free and creative play, in which, in particular, they develop positive social skills and empathy towards each other. The practitioners aid and facilitate the development of life skills over time that then become good habits, supporting the child's learning. Children then become motivated and independent learners.
> — *Steiner Waldorf Framework*

At the outset of Book V, Rousseau carpingly asserted that he aimed to amend Locke's brief address about women's education and, thereby, give it depth and details for the first time (Rousseau, 1974: 321). Nevertheless, Rousseau's position on the education of females is no doubt controversial. In this regard, Mary Wollstonecraft was probably the first key person who criticised Sophie's education in *Emile*, to the extent that the entirety of her book, *A Vindication of the Rights of Woman*, directly condemned Rousseau as deeply biased against women's rights as equal human beings. This chapter aims to outline some of the more significant objections to women's education as illustrated by Rousseau, before we re-interpret (in the next chapter) what he actually meant by Sophie's education and whether his opponents were correct in their disapproval. As such, the first section here summarises the main features of Sophie's education, while the second section sets out the main arguments against this type of education by women's rights advocates both now and then.

Part I: Sophie's Education

The starting point for Sophie's education is that, 'In what they have in common, they are equal. Where they differ, they are not comparable' (Rousseau in Dent, 2005: 118). Each implying, apart from her sexual organs, Sophie is like a man, especially regarding her physical propensities, needs, and emotional faculties (Rousseau, 1974: 321). For Rousseau, the fact that there is a difference in women's sexual body parts (due to their child-bearing capacity) is an indication, above all, that Sophie's moral nature must vary from men (ibid.). Subsequently, Sophie must have all the characteristics required of her sex in order to fulfil her duties in the moral as well as physical order (ibid.), whereby men are envisioned as 'active and strong', whilst women are perceived to be 'passive and weak' (Rousseau in Dent, 2005: 118). Either way, Rousseau does not say that the one is better than the other; but that they are supposed to fulfil different natural positions in society. Certainly, he never maintains to promote Plato's traditional view of turning women into men (Rousseau, 1974: 326). From this point of view, although both sexes strive to a common end (bettering their community, as detailed later on), the means of attaining it must be different for each sex. As such, it would be wrong for the two sexes to occupy functions that *naturally* belong to the other by way of their sexes. In fact, Rousseau refuses to accept that the two sexes are equal, partly because he does not think that a nursing mother's duties would be compatible, say, with the activities inherent in soldiering: 'Can she be a nursing mother to-day and a soldier to-morrow?' (ibid.: 325), predominantly in a context whereon mothers had children with low survival rates in that era (ibid.).

Stated so, it must be noted that the chapter on Sophie does not detail precise stages of development as witnessed in Emile's education, since Rousseau is focused on whatever that is different from Sophie's natural growth as the rest remain the same. In this sense, we have to suppose that Sophie equally follows those stages of development accorded to Emile from the moment of her birth until she marries Emile. Hence, Rousseau agreed that Sophie should develop a strong constitution — in terms of the body — before the cultivation of her mind (ibid.: 329). He thought this was similar to what Spartan girls did in military sports like boys — even though he does not want Sophie to bear sons for war, but rather to give her freedom to develop her physical nature (ibid.: 330). In this fashion, girls should have the ability to play with freedom until they become mothers.

Stated so, unlike Emile, Sophie's education primarily lies with her parents. In short, Rousseau's view of women's specific lessons may be summarised in the following passage. Girls are more ready to do such things, like sewing, cutting out, lace-making, embroidery, and drawing (ibid.: 331). Sophie's education, moreover, must constitute managing the household and its servants, including cooking and cleaning (ibid.: 336). She must learn not to live in extravagance, but maintain modesty (ibid.: 356). Also, she should be able to amuse and charm guests in her husband's house (ibid.: 347). She must be observant and self-possessed (ibid.: 348). Indeed, her education cannot be forced, for she needs to understand the advantages of her domestic duties (ibid.: 349). All in all, she has to develop her taste rather than her talent (ibid.: 357), and become an all-rounder, unlike Emile, who specialises in a single skill (reflected in his choice of vocation): 'she has taste without deep study, talent without art, judgment without learning' (ibid.: 373). In essence, her ideas of the world will be formed not only through readings (which she can learn from her parents), but observations she makes in the 'little world' that she lives in (ibid.: 358). When she has married Emile, he will teach her whatever he has learned himself from his tutor: when this occurs, 'she will not be her husband's teacher but his scholar' (ibid.: 373). Further, when it comes to religion, Sophie must follow the religion of her husband, in the same way that a daughter must follow the religion of her mother before she marries (ibid.: 340).

Throughout her education, although Sophie will be taught 'virtue' very much like Emile, she additionally needs to recognise the significance of other people's judgment: 'when a woman acts well, she has accomplished only half of her task, and what is thought of her is no less important to her than what she actually is' (Rousseau in Dent, 2005: 119-120). Ultimately, this is because Sophie is dependent on Emile: 'she is dependent on our [men's] feelings, on the price we put upon her virtue and the opinion we have of her charms' (Rousseau, 1974: 328). Nonetheless, Rousseau is clear that if there is a conflict between virtue and judgment, the former must prevail. In a sense, she must be the judge of her judges and weigh prejudices at all times before accepting or rejecting them (ibid.: 346). Her 'virtue' — a term not to be understood in the modern sense, as sexual abstinence before marriage, but rather modesty as outlined in the description above regarding a woman's right conduct — would ensure her happiness or '*eudaemonia*'. Hence, without virtue (or '*arete*'), her life would comprise disgrace, unhappiness, shame, and poverty (ibid.: 359).

Essentially, Sophie's education is designed not only to complement Emile's weaknesses, but to provide internal support for his work as a model citizen (ibid.: 328). Nonetheless, as Dent noted, the moral consequences of the differences between the two sexes are not negligible, but may be detrimental for women (Dent, 2005: 118), particularly when Rousseau claimed that they are made for men's delight — men are simply pleasing in themselves, already, by way of their natural strength (Rousseau, 1974: 322); that this is the law of nature, as opposed to any kind of courtship (ibid.). Certainly, in this respect, the moment the two sexes become or imitate the other, they would lose their strength and influence (ibid.: 327). Therewith, in practice, after Sophie has married Emile, she has to live like a nun in a convent, managing the affairs of her household and nursing her children (ibid.: 350). While the young Sophie could take part in festivals, games, coquetry, and other kinds of amusements, a mother and wife, contrastingly, must live in confinement (ibid.).[10] In fact,

---

[10] Incidentally, this is in direct contrast to the traditional way witnessed in France at the time, wherein girls lived in convents first and left when they married (Rousseau, 1974: 350f.). Rousseau believed this latter way had an impoverishing effect on girls' education and turned them into 'little madams' who lacked knowledge of how to conduct themselves well (ibid.: 351).

Rousseau is quick to point out that the structure and operation of a family entirely depend on the wife. For this reason, he emphasises a faithless wife is worse than a faithless husband, because the former 'destroys the family and breaks the bonds of nature' (ibid.: 324).

As an aside, it is worth mentioning that Emile should not be married into a higher family than his (chiefly, in terms of wealth), not only because the wife would have to lower herself to equalise the relationship, but that he could not raise himself to a class above him — primarily because there was no genuine social mobility between the different classes during that period in French history. Henceforth, Rousseau suggested that Sophie must solely marry a husband who is above (or equal to) her family, because in such cases, the husband could easily raise his wife to his level. *Ergo*, when Sophie is ashamed of being poor compared to Emile, she can only confide her secret with the tutor, so that Emile could indirectly find out about Sophie's lack of self-esteem and reassure her of the fact that money does not matter to him!

Against this background, although there appears to be an emphasis on Sophie's subordination to Emile, it is important to highlight that Rousseau thought women were as much able to control men as the other way around (Rousseau in Dent, 2005: 118). In this connexion, Rousseau believed that a woman's strength was in her charms by means of which she compelled men to use their strength — that is to say, not only by exciting their passions beyond their ability to satisfy them, but also through her resistance to the husband's imploration (Rousseau, 1974: 322-323). Figuratively speaking, she is like the eyes of a body, and man its hands (ibid.: 340).[11] To this end, on the whole, Sophie would need to have a good knowledge of her husband's mind (ibid.: 350). In this fashion, it goes without saying, a man who was being cruel to his wife would sooner

---

[11] Interestingly, such descriptions are very similar to a variety of novels published following Rousseau's era, including Jane Austen's *Pride and Prejudice* and Charlotte Brontë's *Jane Eyre*, in which a stoic, albeit charming young governess, managing the affairs of Mr Rochester's household, both excites his passions, while resisting his advances until an appropriate occasion presents itself.

or later yield to her gentleness and follow her commands — perhaps in the same way that Hercules spun at the feet of Omphale (ibid.: 334). Nevertheless, in spite of the fact women have the influence to rule men, she must still be obedient to her husband and remain subordinate: 'Woman is made to yield to man and to endure even his injustice' — much unlike a man, who will rise and revolt, if forced into subordination (Rousseau in Dent, 2005: 120).

Certainly, therewith, when Emile is separated from Sophie as he approaches the last stage of his development, Sophie is obliged to wait for him and continue her education as before. Her days, howbeit, are now spent thinking of Emile and his safety as he travels the world. When he returns, this attitude will extend to the entirety of her life, in that even when Emile's sexual passion is cooled, Sophie must show great devotion and remain a lover with him for the rest of his life (Rousseau, 1974: 440). With this said, Sophie needs to recognise that her duties are the basis of her rights and the source of her pleasures (ibid.: 353). In that sense, Rousseau contended, nature determines specific roles for each sex, which they must adhere to if they are to retain their natural rights (Dent, 2005: 118).

On the whole, notwithstanding the fact Rousseau believed his ideas were according to human nature, as he observed, significant criticisms have followed the publication of *Emile*. The rest of this chapter examines some of the more important critiques of women's education as defined by Rousseau.

Part II: Received Criticisms

Perhaps Rousseau's most ardent critic following *Emile* was Mary Wollstonecraft, whose chief concern was true equality between men and women. In this instance, she opposed the idea that from the time of their infancy, women should be told to follow certain rules and practical guidelines in order to obtain men's protection: rules such as possessing 'a little knowledge of human weakness (properly called "cunning"), softness of temperament, outward obedience, and scrupulous attention to a puerile kind of propriety' (Wollstonecraft, 2017: 13). Accordingly, she rejected all prevalent notions of contrast between the two sexes, stating that both men and women are human beings with an identical capacity to reason (or rationality). As such, things like dressing for alluring men were not 'natural' to women but arose from a love of power within men; which possibly demonstrates why she was critical of such statements by Rousseau as, '[e]ducate women like men [...] and the more they resemble our sex, the less power will they have over us' (Rousseau in ibid.: 43). Quintessentially, Rousseau thought, inauthentic pedagogies could only lead to a weakening of each sex's power and influence, which would thereby destabilise the natural social order betwixt men and women. What is more, by being waylaid from their natural inclinations, differing types of social chaos would emerge, in which the 'general will' could sink into particularity through Sophie's inability to ensure Emile's rightful conduct towards the general good of their society (as discussed above).

In this context, Wollstonecraft maintained, '[i]f women are in general feeble in body and mind, that arises less from nature than from education' (ibid.: 28). Therefore, she continued, dolls would never have interested girls, in the first place, if they had not been confined to inactivity or whose innocence had been 'tainted by false shame' (ibid.: 30). In short, girls were allowed 'no *serious* occupations' (originally emphasised by the author), and they were always left with the pursuit of pleasure (ibid.: 35). Wollstonecraft, by so positing, argued that women's education, in particular their 'upbringing and situation' (ibid.: 2), limited the female sex's faculty to fulfil its potential and turned them to frivolous, slavish mistresses; thus withdrawing their freedom and giving rise to unintelligent, ignorant, unaffectionate, promiscuous and ineffective mothers — rather than the contrary. What is worse, women's education seemed to encourage them to become somewhat immoral and selfish creatures.

Consecutively, Wollstonecraft rejected the notion that an equal education would lead to 'masculine women'. To her mind, the most perfect education was one that enabled 'the individual to attain such habits of virtue as will render him or her independent' (ibid.: 14); otherwise, we would only have 'overgrown children' (ibid.: 15). Either way, she believed one way that could prove if differences between men and women were 'natural' would be to design an equal, coeducational system that gave both sexes equal opportunities from birth. In any event, the word 'natural' seems to be inflicted with a problematic definition. Indeed, while Rousseau intended that both men and women attain their 'natural' state by following certain steps, the issue is that Rousseau did not clarify what he meant by this state. Certainly, he said the pursuit of the 'natural' leads to happiness and self-fulfilment. But, then, one could question the parameters of happiness as well as what a term like 'happiness' would actually mean inside that behavioural context. When all is said and done, questions concerning both long-term and short-term happiness immediately arise along with one's personal capacities or failings to achieve these social and psychological factors. It goes without saying, one is reminded of the differences outlined by Mill between pleasure and happiness in relation to 'utility' — a topic, which was discussed latterly, but never directly by Rousseau himself.

Against this backdrop, Wollstonecraft inevitably viewed Sophie as 'grossly unnatural' (ibid.: 16), living the role of a plaything who had to entertain Emile whenever he wanted to relax. This idea of women, no doubt, is perhaps exemplified in Rousseau's following statement in his autobiography: 'The freshness of her flesh, the brightness of her colouring, the whiteness of her teeth, the sweetness of her breath, the air of cleanliness that pervades her person' — a description of one of the many ladies he fell in love with during his lifetime (Rousseau, 1953: 301). All the same, Wollstonecraft noted, '[w]hen the husband stopped being a lover — and that time will inevitably come — her desire to please will weaken, or become a spring of bitterness; and love, perhaps the least durable of all the passions, will give place to jealousy or vanity' (Wollstonecraft, 2017: 18). Each reflection demonstrating the radical contrast of opinion existing between Wollstonecraft and Rousseau. Undoubtedly, in this way, she argued women could not be limited to domestic concerns, or forced into a passive role, which did not actively engage with their society as model citizens alongside men. Doing so would illogically disable half the world's population from contributing to the progress of civilisation and humanity, not to forget any involvement in the state as parliamentary representatives.

That said, as another point of reference contra Sophie's education, it is also useful to briefly examine one of J. S. Mill's most grounded works, *The Subjection of Women*, as a founding text on liberal feminism; for, regardless of some similarities in argumentation with Wollstonecraft, Mill's essay provides an even clearer extrapolation in defence of women's equal rights. Accordingly, from his standpoint, Mill is not concerned with great men, but only with bad ones. In other words, although he does not doubt the great goodness, happiness, and affection of an absolute government under a good man, he is worried that these cases are far too rare compared to a majority who tyrannise their power; and that it is these specific instances which Mill wants to prevent from occurring.

Overall, Mill's assertion was that perceptions of women's weaker and subordinate nature primarily arose from inherited custom. In this sense, perceptions were essentially assumed in theory rather than observed in reality or even through trial and error: in a court of law, 'the burthen of proof is supposed to lie with the affirmative' (Mill, 1991: 472). In fact, according to Mill, from early history, the subordination of the weaker sex arose from women's dependence on some men due to her inferiority in muscular strength and the value attached to her by men. Mill, moreover, took problem with the fact that women's subordination is due to men wanting to maintain their power in domestic life (ibid.: 524). Nevertheless, he equally noted that women's independence not only seemed more natural to the Greeks than other ancients at the time, but, in point of fact, Queen Elizabeth, Deborah, and Joan of Arc, amongst others, demonstrated firmness and vigour of their rule, not to forget intelligence (ibid.: 529). In this context, the *a priori* assumption is freedom and impartiality, and, most importantly, the retention of a healthy scepticism and spirit of inquiry without which one's personal judgment will always vindicate traditional viewpoints.

Against that backdrop, Mill's defence of women's equality may be divided into the social and the individual. Regarding the former, Mill proposed two principal benefits arising from equality: expediency and justice. In connection with expediency, it may only be said that by refusing one-half of humanity to participate with freedom in society, people are simply denied access to the benefits of competition: namely, the adoption of best processes by the most qualified agents in solving problems leading to the common good. Competition, accordingly, would be a stimulating factor for both sexes; or, as a matter of course, the strengths of both sexes could combine for even better results. (ibid.: 535). With reference to justice, Mill questioned the refusal of women's 'fair share of honour and distinction, or […] the equal moral right of all human beings to choose their occupation' (ibid.: 526). For Mill, to be sure, justice simply demanded moral equality for all human beings.

That observed, concerning the individual, Mill thought of three specific advantages. Firstly, within the family, the ideal of marriage is when both sexes improve one another; that a woman who is intellectually inferior (due to her education) will undermine and degenerate the husband. The second is about freedom and the fact it is the only means by which one could become happy personally: indeed, as Mill stated, 'freedom is the first and strongest want of human nature' after food and raiment (ibid.: 576). Thirdly, bringing down the barriers of inequality would not only expand women's faculties but their range of moral sentiments as well (ibid.: 563). Therefore, Mill believed women could gain, individually, a combination of the three benefits outlined if they had equality with men.

That stated, delving into recent criticisms, they are more concerned with details of Rousseau's exposition as opposed to overarching theoretical counter-arguments, as observed in Wollstonecraft and Mill. For instance, Darling and Pijpekamp maintain that critics often underestimate Rousseau's view of women's education. According to both authors, Rousseau not only refuses to take umbrage with the abuse of women by men, but rather seems to legitimise it, either as a form of punishment or because he refuses to believe women's declarations about not wanting to have sex (Darling and Pijpekamp, 1994: 117). Certainly, it may be stated, this is evident in various examples throughout the chapter on Sophie: the main case in point being Rousseau's statement that even if a man treats his wife with cruelty and injustice, the woman should submit and suffer the wrongs, hoping her tender and gentle attitude would soften her husband's disposition. Fundamentally, a woman's main duty is to fulfil the needs of men only, in spite of any pain or suffering afflicted therefrom.

Furthermore, as Jimack pointed out, it is not clear what Rousseau meant by the claim that 'the first impulses of *nature* [emphasis added] are always right' (Rousseau in Jimack, 1974: xviii). Put differently, trust in 'nature' is a question of definition because what Rousseau considered to be 'good' was also 'natural'. It is for this reason, Rousseau viewed laziness, vice, and cruelty as unnatural, since they cannot be good. He believed unnatural characteristics had to be corrected or prevented by way of appropriate education, particularly in one's early childhood. Either way, according to Jimack, because of his belief in natural goodness, Rousseau appears to have had fewer pedagogical reservations than might be expected since this view did not 'blind him to the existence of what other people might term natural faults' (ibid.: xix). Discussed simply, Rousseau appears blinkered to the fact that there are natural failings as well as natural goods, whilst every natural impulse is not necessarily of benefit to a human being. All meaning, one must be hesitant regarding Rousseau's definition of 'nature' or, for that matter, how he could discover its aspects.

What is more, Paul Thomas is critical of the interrelationship between Rousseau's views on sexuality and politics. Indeed, upon closer inspection, the apparent link between the two fields is that the 'general will' or the corresponding symmetry between subject and sovereign in the community (debated in the first chapter) is not possible without the existence of women as a specific proportion of the population supporting husbands who are supposed to be actively involved in the political arena. Viewed in terms of the public and private divide, thus, the duty of the wife in the private domain is to ensure that her husband is consoled, solaced and comforted as well as encouraged to participate effectively in the public or political arena, and in so doing prevent not only his corruption, but also repressing his '*amour-propre*' (pride) at the same time. Apparently, Thomas holds, while this indicates the significance and interdependence of the two sexes on one another, the relationship is unequal in that women are merely confined indoors and by this means only live at the margins of politics. In a way, while civic equality lies amongst men, domestic inequality lies between men and women.

Relevantly, it is sometimes claimed Sophie's education is oriented towards making Emile whole, at the expense of her own, leaving her in a state of conflict (Schaeffer, 1998: 609). Specifically, it is argued that because Sophie is insufficiently integrated into the communal wholeness or the 'general will' (ibid.: 609), she is bound to undermine Rousseau's overall goal of wholeness in the family by fostering a sense of inequality between Sophie and Emile. Hence, although Rousseau stated he was committed to Sophie's integrity, in theory, the patriarchal relationship between her and Emile undermines her integrity in practice (ibid.: 614).

Lastly, it goes without saying, although an apologist may state that Rousseau was, ultimately, a creature of his time and could not avoid certain conclusions about the role of women in society, not unlike the slaves of ancient Greece who could not participate in democratic processes, it is said that Rousseau did not see himself as a creature of his own time since he always tried to propound thoughts that were against popular opinion or an uninformed *vox populi* (Dent, 2005: 117). This point perhaps cannot be made any clearer by the fact the entirety of his other works contained views in radical contrast to the ideas of his day (ibid.: 117). All meaning, it is surprising Rousseau did not apply his radicalism to women's education.

Conclusion

To sum, although there are certain similarities between Sophie and Emile's education, the differences are assuredly striking. Sophie's education is designed to keep her housebound, Emile's is to enable him to freely roam the world; Sophie must become a passive nurturer, Emile the active provider; the list goes on, doubtless. Thus, by today's standards, Rousseau may simply appear to have prejudiced views about women's role in society, no matter what their education. In certain respects, this has substantially impacted *Emile*'s reception as a key text in the Philosophy of Education today. Nonetheless, despite the importance of the above-mentioned criticisms, it could be argued that Rousseau's oeuvre is largely misunderstood, particularly when considering his unique manner of argumentation. The next chapter aims to offer a few fresh perspectives that better shed light on Sophie's education.

IV. A DEFENCE OF ROUSSEAU

> When approached by the news media and asked the question, 'What did Waldorf education do for you?' I replied, 'It encouraged me to always strive to become a better human being.
> — *Jens Stoltenberg, Former Prime Minister of Norway*

This chapter aims to re-interpret Rousseau's views on feminine education in order to clarify his writings about women's characteristics and role in society. For this purpose, the first part here will set out the argument that Sophie is, in fact, superior to Emile, according to Denise Schaeffer. The second part will maintain that Sophie's education results in equality with Emile, as propounded by Penny Weiss. However, the most original contribution of this entire dissertation to current literature in this field is within the second half of this part, wherein we will briefly trace Rousseau's thoughts through the writings of a few key authors he mentioned in his corpus, including Homer, Plato, and Daniel Defoe. It goes without saying, although a defence of Rousseau usually appears apologetic, Sophie's education must be understood within the broader framework of his theory. As such, both parts will take into account Rousseau's broader philosophy, politics, and education as set out in the previous chapters of this thesis.

Part I: Sophie's Superiority

Schaeffer's main focus of attention regarding Sophie's superiority is 'wholeness', or 'the absence of internal conflict or division' within her as an individual citizen (Schaeffer, 1998: 608). To begin with, Rousseau believed that the equilibrium for 'wholeness' could only be maintained either in the state of nature or in a model city consisting of citizens who identified themselves with the 'general will' (ibid.). With that in mind, although the 'wholeness' of the family is different from the 'wholeness' found in savage people or model citizens, it is the sole viable option when one cannot recover the independence that characterises the state of nature, or when the private and public realms of society leave individuals in a 'divided state' (ibid.). That being said, it is important to note that 'the interdependent wholeness of the family is not achieved when two radically self-sufficient individuals are fused together' (ibid.: 614).

As such, while *amour-propre*, which results in dependency on others, appears to be encouraged in the education of girls, Rousseau envisioned it 'as inimical to a unified soul' in Sophie (ibid.: 610). As a point of evidence, Schaeffer notes that Sophie's supposed 'divided soul' makes her more complex than Emile, as a model that entails both self-rule at the same time as non-authoritarian rule of others (ibid.: 607). In other words, Sophie's 'divided soul' is due to her independence rather than any type of subordination to Emile (ibid.: 610). In this way, Sophie does not undermine the community through her dividedness, but becomes vital to the continued existence of a familial community, much like a legislator in a political community managing the 'general will' (ibid.: 610). Put simply, without Sophie, Emile would not have the familial basis to effectively participate in his community.

Being independent, Sophie is the only person who is able to recognise Emile's *amour-propre* and how to guide it. This aspect of Sophie and Emile's relationship is best indicated when she challenges Emile to a race. In this instance, Sophie understands Emile and controls his *amour-propre* via arousing his vanity and allowing him to take the lead towards the finish line (even though he eventually helps Sophie win by slowing down), thereby setting 'the order of the relationship in motion' (ibid.: 617). In this context, she is not ordered, but the one who orders (ibid.), like a philosopher king whose 'noble lie' is consciously directed in order to enact objectives that benefit the society (ibid.: 618).

It is for this reason, while some may say that men's 'direct (publicly sanctioned) rule will always be more powerful than indirect rule', the means to achieving a harmonious balance of power, or 'wholeness' in the family, will require a certain degree of imbalance, which can only come from Sophie (Schaeffer: 616). Rulings, thus, require certain knowledge on the part of Sophie, but unrecognised by Emile, to maintain the coherence of the whole (ibid.: 618). The only difference between Sophie and the tutor or legislator, in this context, is that she is a part of this whole, and therefore her education should allow her to comprehend and transcend it — so, her education cannot simply be complementary to Emile's (ibid.: 618).

On a related note, it is also worth mentioning the fact that Rousseau never takes away wit or truth from women, but adds another dimension to their education through physical attractiveness: in this way, supposedly '[f]eminine traits are added to masculine traits, and may often disguise them, but do not displace them' (ibid.: 613). At the same time, notwithstanding, moral and rational judgments are expected of women, as of men, so they may see the bigger picture (ibid.); hence, Rousseau's statement, '[a]s soon as she depends on both her own conscience and the opinions of others, she has to learn these two rules, to reconcile them, and to prefer the former only when the two are in contradiction' (Rousseau in ibid.). With this in mind, Sophie must be able to compare internal as well as external dictates; and use that knowledge to know when to lead Emile or when to follow him (ibid.: 614). Thus, while there may be concerns that Rousseau's encouragement of women's apparent subjugation can lead to their actual subordination, the fact he wants Sophie to be smarter, more independent, and more powerful (albeit indirectly) than Emile, makes her an elevated individual to him (ibid.: 615f.). This is on the assumption, of course, that independence is equated, for Rousseau, with superiority, because, at the end of the day, he maintained that independence viewed as a form of freedom ennobles a human being, whilst being a God-given natural right (as validated in the first chapter).

Anyway, a relevant issue that needs to be addressed is whether Sophie is happy with her condition. According to Schaeffer, the notion of happiness in *Emile* seems to undergo a change from an equilibrium between desire and faculty to the added dimension of personal responsibility (ibid.: 618). After all, in reality, Rousseau was particularly pessimistic about achieving happiness under the limitations of our human condition, or, for that matter, combining happiness with freedom, as witnessed in the state of nature (ibid.: 625). As such, if happiness is to exist internally, he maintained, Sophie must have self-consciousness. Yet, as this is likely to disrupt the balance between desire and faculty, she must be able to stand outside the whole, hold it together and be her own tutor concurrently in order to be free (ibid.: 620). Indeed, this is in contrast to 'the girl like Sophie' (a second Sophie introduced by Rousseau later in the chapter) who seeks perfection in her mate in the image of Telemachus, the brave protagonist of Fenelon's *The Adventures of Telemachus* — a novel which she reads fervently (ibid.: 615). All meaning, the second Sophie cannot allow herself to submit to a whole that is not perfect (ibid.: 620). Rousseau believes this is a tragedy as 'the girl like Sophie' will remain perpetually 'outside' this whole and will never be able to feel love for Emile (ibid.: 621); whereas the first (real) Sophie could exist both within and without the relationship at once.

Parenthetically, at any rate, this is why she has the independence to choose her mate, while Emile's choice is greatly influenced by his tutor before he meets Sophie (ibid.: 615): Sophie, as her own tutor, can draw conclusions according to her judgment of whether Emile compares with her actual ideal; that is to say, one who possesses integrity and virtue (Dent, 2005: 120). As a matter of course, this is relevant to balancing emotional and moral inequality for the purpose of maintaining equality and mutual affection, rather than a ruler-ruled partnership. At this point, Schaeffer observes that Sophie seeks a mate who possesses a self-consciousness like her (Schaeffer, 1998: 622). In the long run, this is because she does not want to rule tyrannically; instead, she wishes Emile to be self-ruling and virtuous (ibid.: 622); a fact distinctly evidenced when Sophie accepted Emile's marriage proposal only after Emile had told her he would never give up the rights of humanity even if she were the arbiter of his life (ibid.).

Either way, lastly, while Rousseau aims to expose internal tensions in human relationships, one finds that Emile's education, in the long run, is insufficient in comparison to Sophie, when in *Emile et Sophie* (unfinished sequel to *Emile*), the connection between the two is undermined after the exposition that Sophie had partaken in an extramarital affair. In this matter, it must be mentioned, Emile is not aware that her action was due to the distress caused by the death of people around her. As such, Schaeffer argues, had Emile been more sophisticated and better understood the complexities of our human soul, it would have been unlikely for him to abandon Sophie. Therefore, the issue is that Emile is not like Sophie and cannot conceive that Sophie might have an 'imperfection' — aside from the fact her imperfection is necessary and inevitable, bearing in mind her divided soul — which is, so to speak, why he cannot accept her unfaithful action, or advertently choose the real over the imaginary ideal (ibid.: 624).

What Emile and Sophie share is a tension which both need to submit to, and transcend for the purpose of holding the whole together (ibid.: 264f.). Further, this tension would encourage them to 'self-overcome' on another level — for virtue and love (ibid.: 625). Still, under these rubrics, only Sophie is aware of the problem. So, while Emile's freedom is ensured by the framework within which he experiences love and family life (through subjection to Sophie), Sophie's freedom is linked with her imperfection — because, in this instance, 'perfection and illusion are aligned against freedom' (ibid.). What Sophie tells us is a flaw in Rousseau's depiction of perfection in regards to the 'general will', in that a lack of a 'Sophie-like figure' in the polity makes it difficult to distinguish between radical democracy and tyranny in the 'ideal regime' (ibid.: 626).

All things considered, Sophie and Emile's relationship 'is neither a perfect whole with two complementary parts, nor a strict hierarchy', because otherwise, the relationship would be too static, and they could not accommodate the instability involved in the interdependence between each other (ibid.: 624). In this sense, with regards to 'wholeness', Emile has the same problem as Sophie in that both need to exist inside and outside of themselves, with the only difference that Emile is not aware of this issue, unlike Sophie (ibid.).

Be that as it may, although this section demonstrates that Sophie may be seen as Emile's superior, Schaeffer's argument in regards to Sophie's superiority is still apologetic since it does not wholly address the personal injustices inherent in her social and domestic position regardless of her assumed pre-eminence sketched above. Furthermore, there may be disagreement regarding the need to view Sophie as Emile's superior, as opposed to both being equal. As such, the next section puts Emile and Sophie amid a particular cultural milieu to demonstrate that Rousseau's view of women is a result of the historical period within which the characters find themselves — as opposed to any set of eternal verities — as may be deduced following a textual reading of Rousseau. On the whole, it is contended that in Rousseau's mind, harmony in society requires certain dedicated roles for each citizen.

Part II: Sophie and Emile as Equals

To start with, Penny A. Weiss has another interpretation of Sophie's education, which is both noteworthy as well as interesting. In short, while 'Rousseau is clearly an advocate of sex roles', therewith supporting women's confinement to the private sphere, duties of wife and mother, and the supposed indirect access to power, Weiss' contention is that there are actually no natural differences between the two sexes, but that they are 'created, encouraged, and enforced' to ensure they perform their proper social function (Weiss, 1987: 83). Therefore, Weiss does not assume the two sexes possess radically dissimilar natures as defined by Rousseau (ibid.: 82). By contrast, their natures are malleable (ibid.: 83), probably according to the 'general will' or the society within which they exist. Put differently, Weiss asserts, a clear distinction must occur between the 'is' of sex differences and the 'ought' of different social roles (ibid.). This, transparently, makes her argument negative (as a mere defence of Sophie's education, not its active promotion).

Either way, Weiss reasons, there are four specific aspects that appear to indicate equivalence between the two sexes: physical strength, mental capacities, reproduction, interests, and dispositions (ibid.: 84ff.). Regarding the first, Weiss argues, no distinctions are indicated between men and women on the basis of strength, since Rousseau did not *originally* find them weak (as showcased in his discussion of 'noble savages' in his first two discourses), but rather he *wanted* to make them weak, which manifestly would render women incapable of soldiering or other such tasks traditionally associated with men (ibid.: 85). From this standpoint, the 'savage woman's ability' to fight against others and the elements in order to protect herself and her children is striking and demonstrates her physical strength in comparison to men. In this context, Weiss reasons, Rousseau suggested that men within the current social order would ideally be defenders of their families and general community, while women's induced weaknesses in terms of physical strength (endurance and so on) would motivate them to complete 'social tasks' which might remain unfinished otherwise (ibid.: 86). Everything considered, these prescribed roles would be for the benefit of others in the wider society (ibid.: 86).

Regarding mental capacities, whilst others like Aristotle believed that women were naturally inferior because their 'deliberative faculty' functioned 'in a form which remains inconclusive' (Aristotle in ibid.: 86f.), nowhere is it stated that Rousseau subscribed to a similar outlook (ibid.: 87), or that there were any limits on either sex's intellectual development (ibid.: 87). Contrastingly, Rousseau not only admits women have rationality, as evidenced in his description of well-read, cultured, curious, and intelligent women in his *Confessions*, he never states that the 'higher' rational function — traditionally associated with men — is out of women's reach, but the singular lack of comparable intellectual contributions on the part of women is largely the result of an education that deprives women of such tuition. Arguably, Weiss maintains regarding Rousseau's theme, even if women were tutored in such a fashion, he conjectured that such things as the sciences (which involve rational thinking) have had a negative impact on morals and politics, whilst offering no guarantee of well-being either personally or socially — as demonstrated in the first chapter (ibid.: 87). Hence, the 'noble savage', being his ideal, Rousseau never extolled the virtues of cold, objective reasoning (ibid.: 88).

Characteristically, this view is perhaps demonstrated by the fact Rousseau was dramatically obsessed with almost every single woman he met in his life, even though timidity and shyness typified most of his interactions (Rousseau, 1953: 25ff.), while his natural hyper-sensitivity encouraged him to care deeply for each (ibid.: 37f.). In fact, his view of women is probably best witnessed by his treatment of Mme de Warens as his primary love interest (or his potential Sophie). Illustratively, in the two weeks before his death, he stated in his final writing that, 'I only lived in and for her' (Rousseau in Butterworth, 1992: 140). As such, what is, for the most part, remarkable in his description of this relationship is the close intimacy and love described. The reason why this is important is that as a Romantic, he valued emotion or instinct above rationality: 'Rousseau thought and wrote about thinking to draw others away from the pernicious effects of thinking and to bring them back into closer harmony with their own feelings' (ibid.: 152). This implies, in turn, the relationship between Emile and Sophie was more based on private harmony than a contractual partnership.

In this sense, Rousseau's 'functionalist' approach to women's education more or less attempted to distinguish 'between what women *can* learn and what they *ought* to learn' (Weiss, 1987: 88). He ultimately believed that different education systems ensure an interdependence between the two sexes, which overcomes their natural 'asociability' as individuals (ibid.: 89). This is on the pretext of the belief that happiness is a balance between ability and desire (ibid.: 89), in that one must limit one's desires to what is within reach, never beyond, to preserve their overall happiness.

With that in our sights, the third subject matter is regarding reproduction. According to Weiss, Rousseau does not think sentiment or attachment is unique to women, especially as it is understood in the form of 'maternal instinct' (ibid.: 90). Instead, it arises from continuous living with children (ibid.). It is only with the evolution of society and the rise of the family as a useful tool that divisions emerge in social roles. In this sense, the family becomes important for Rousseau both to preserve public morality, and to ensure people's participation in and loyalty to the state for its well-being (ibid.: 91). In this setting, women serve as a link between men and children, ensuring that the former loves the latter.

At any rate, the fourth aspect demonstrating equality between the sexes relates to interests and dispositions. Specifically, Weiss observes that to Rousseau's mind, boys were only immune from the opinions of others — unlike girls as perceived then — because they were independent and were able to have pleasure at all times (ibid.: 93). But, Rousseau also admitted, it was entirely possible that with enough time and effort, boys could equally become 'subjected to the same law' that governed girls (ibid.: 92f.). Similarly, with regards to interests, it should not be forgotten that Rousseau's view of savage women was, in any manner of speaking, at odds with Sophie's love of jewels, paints, and flowers (ibid.: 93): savage women, in other words, were no different from savage men.

Although the four aspects above show how Sophie may be equal to Emile, the arguments are nevertheless negative and still apologetic, for they do not positively promote the historical significance of the social roles that Rousseau advocated for women. For starters, as observed in the first chapter, the significance of societal harmony for Rousseau is plainly evidenced by his emphasis on the duty of every citizen to adopt one's state religion, whatever it may be: 'since I wished to become a citizen I must become a Protestant and return to the established faith of my country' as Rousseau wrote in his autobiography (Rousseau, 1953: 366). Overall, this is because he believed that everything emerges from politics and that 'no people would ever be other than the nature of their government made them' (ibid.: 377); essentially, politics affects the domestic life of families.

Hence, if the 'sovereign' decided a relationship like Sophie and Emile is ideal for social order, then that is what would be required of individuals within that community; just like the fact, Rousseau reconverted to Protestantism (from Catholicism) when he returned to his home country. Rousseau's belief in this ideal was made clear in this statement: '[the] general objectives of all institutions must be modified in each country to meet local conditions and suit the character of the people concerned' (Rousseau, 1968: 97). All that implies, customs, beliefs, and morals must vary with the climate of every 'body politic' (ibid.: 128): culture for Athens, trade for Carthage and Tyre, seafaring for Rhodes, War for Sparta, and civic virtue for Rome (ibid.: 98). The 'Lawgiver', put differently, is responsible for directing the constitution towards ends in concordance with the demands of circumstances. (ibid.: 98). After all, Rousseau himself upheld that in the 'state of savagery', both sexes are 'undifferentiated', whereas, in civilized life, their characteristics have been developed by social institutions (Rousseau, 1974: 368).

That, however, leads to questions about the effects of customs on people's relationships with one another, as well as how they would be different or similar in other societies. Confessed so, this is an important discussion mainly due to the fact Rousseau was influenced by ancient Greece and Rome, where homosexuality and pederasty were norms. To elaborate, according to the pundits of that time, including Plato, in certain Greek city-states, like Sparta, the preponderance of homosexual relationships was nothing unusual (Plato, 1998: 12), but rather something helping to explain the manifest intimacy shared betwixt such Greek heroes as Achilles and Patroclus in Homer's *The Iliad* (Homer, 1966). Indeed, this is equally evidenced by Hanson's (2009: 124) comment regarding Sparta: 'the separation of the sexes at any early age, together with attitudes peculiar to other Greeks on the role of women, resulted in overtly homosexual relationships centring on life in the barracks'; or, in other words, an official status for such inclinations inside a militarist state. To be more precise, Rousseau's sense of love is palpably in line with 'platonic' love (Waterfield, 1998: xi), or, otherwise stated, the Socratic definition of friendship or *'philia'*, found in the *Lysis* (one of Socrates' early dialogues), not to mention *Symposium*, which is hardly surprising when considering that Williams tellingly concludes there is a compelling engagement between Rousseau and Platonism, overall: 'indeed [he is] one of the "greatest and most consistent Platonists of the modern era"' (Williams in Hanley, 2010: 1). Positively, in the context of the homosexual relationship between Hippothales, the *'erastēs'* (the older and sexually active partner) and Lysis, the *'paidika'* (the younger sexually passive partner), Socrates noted that *'philia'* was supposed to have an educative role in that the 'good' partner — in the sense proposed in the Socratic dialogues as just and self-sufficient — had to be desired by one who was 'neither good nor bad' and who wanted to become 'good' like his older friend (Watt, 1987: 119). According to Socrates, also, the 'good' person cannot love another who is also 'good' because both individuals are quintessentially good (or 'godlike') and would not be in need of one another. This tantalisingly suggests why Rousseau believed Emile's education had to involve what Sophie's could not in order to ensure the two could complement each other: Emile as the 'good' (self-sufficient) individual to be loved by the passive (dependent) Sophie who was 'neither good nor bad'. What is interesting here is that even Wollstonecraft admitted where *real* love is involved in an intimate relationship between man and woman, different sexes could be treated distinctly as opposed to purely equally (Wollstonecraft, 2017: 39).

Anyhow, freedom must be applicable to every person in Rousseau's understanding of people's relationships, which is why what makes all the difference is his emphasis on the significance of individual roles, roles found in society as a result of its varied history. When reading about Sophie's education, then, we must bear in mind that Rousseau was writing a treatise for the people of France, according to his understanding of this society, as opposed to others.[12] Thus, the relationship between Emile and Sophie is the creature of an ideal 'general will' that Rousseau thought had to be adopted by the French people of that era. In this manner of speaking, in another society, a younger man could take the place of Sophie, whilst a woman could take the place of Emile and so on. The only caveat to be borne in mind is that he did not theorise beyond his own society, or for that matter, its future.

The word 'nature', in accordance, was probably a rhetorical device used by Rousseau, which was intended to have a persuasive effect on his readers. Indeed, as Weiss (1987: 93) pointed out, Rousseau viewed human nature as malleable as well as 'that which is useful in a given situation'. All suggesting, Rousseau must be understood in the normative sense, rather than the descriptive. And although he admits to not being thoroughly clear about differences in sex, his discussions of inequality develop, in the first place, because of the importance he gives to the sexual division for the purpose of social unity (ibid.: 95). Either way, it must be distinguished that Rousseau's rhetoric undercuts his theoretical arguments primarily as a way of coaxing readers into general agreement. By this reasoning, one should be mindful of the form rather than the subject matter of *Emile*, for Rousseau's eloquence and lapidary phrasing were intended to move the reader's heart, even if that meant something of an exaggeration. In this vein, there is an interesting comment by Kerber in the possibility that 'Rousseau's conservatism about women may well have served to make his radical comments about

---

[12] In his autobiography, Rousseau records that *Emile* would not have been read or understood by English people due to their different culture and way of understanding, in comparison to the French.

men's behaviour more palatable' (Thomas, 1991: 196-197). Apart from that, moreover, not unlike a legislator in *The Social Contract*, he uses 'the always-respectable and always-nebulous language of nature' to ensure the fulfilment of social functions (ibid.: 94). 'Noble lies' (in this instance, sex roles), consequently, may be viewed as one of Rousseau's rhetorical techniques (ibid.).

Lastly, regarding his use of rhetoric, it is wise to remember that *Emile* as a novel was composed to win over and persuade reasonably educated audiences to Rousseau's ideas through characters and dramatic settings, rather than formal arguments, expounding the rightness or wrongness of specific propositions. To be sure, this was apt amid the turbulent backdrop of conventional views in the eighteenth century, which perpetually sought to defend themselves against any type of radicalism and adaptation.

Conclusion

The most obvious defence of Rousseau's proposed education for women is that he was the first to give any semblance of importance to the feminine gender and their education. This point is best demonstrated by one of John Locke's (1824: 6ff.) influential books on education, *Some Thoughts Concerning Education*, in which he highlighted the importance of giving freedom to the body, employing the services of a long-term tutor, developing resilience against the passions of the body, amongst other lessons. Having stated that, Locke's main focus of attention was boys' education, which is why he totally ignored girls' education through the entirety of his book, except for briefly supporting equality between the two sexes (Simons, 1990: 140). By contrast, no thanks to being one of the few authors who dedicated significant portions of his written work to women, Rousseau's rhetorical style distinguished him from other writers, while his extrapolations on women's education was a new development at the time for openly discussing women's lives, if not their nature. When assessed in this way, one is less likely to be critical of Rousseau, as the first author who gave women a voice in the written discourses of that period.

In parallel, it has been argued that Rousseau himself was not free from prejudice, something perhaps portrayed by his false suspicion that his friends, namely David Hume and Diderot, attempted to 'poison' him after he had become famous. In this circumstance, it is advocated that Rousseau was equally susceptible to committing mistakes, like any other human being, and could not possibly create a prejudice-free theory of women's education. After all, even Wollstonecraft, who ardently criticised Rousseau, appeared to promote the eighteenth-century notion of child-rearing as a vital role for *every* woman (Darling and Pijpekamp, 1994: 121). All things considered, although such arguments may appear to defend Rousseau at a glance, they do not offer a satisfactory account of his theory.

In which instance, delving into more fundamental issues, this chapter examined Sophie's superiority or equality in relation to Emile, according to the writings of two authors, Schaeffer and Weiss, respectively. Overall, it was observed that such arguments are, in the same vein as the above, apologetic (characteristically) as opposed to anything positive. Hence, after exploring the broader context of Rousseau's idea of love, it was argued that Sophie's education was a result of France's socio-political context when it was written, which is why it was probably appropriate to that period and place. All meaning, one could actively promote and defend Sophie's education within Rousseau's society, keeping in mind that the 'general will' ultimately determines the social roles which individuals must fulfil within their relationship for the overall benefit of society. So, from here on, we will summarise and conclude the topic of this dissertation.

FINAL THOUGHTS

> We are all stars but we must learn how to shine.
> — *Marylin Monroe, American Actress, Model and Singer*

As Wokler (2001: 99) mentioned, '[n]o other political thinker, ancient or modern, was in that period more venerated than Rousseau'. In fact, 'his *Social Contract* would in the course of the French Revolution come to be esteemed as if [it] formed the Ten Commandments of the new Republic of France' (ibid.: 98). Apart from that, Rousseau's influence (certainly, alongside Dewey) on 'progressive education' in the last century could not be stressed any more strongly — even though it is now diminishing slowly. Still and all, Rousseau is a highly controversial figure, especially because his views are often grossly misrepresented. After all, as Dent (2005: 118) pointed out, in spite of the fact he advocated that it was the duty of women to please and delight men in *Emile*, Rousseau criticised 'lascivious' habits as being unnatural, in the first place. Similarly, to be more precise, despite speaking of dependence, Rousseau advocated attachment for men and women as opposed to the former in order to maintain one's freedom (Rousseau, 1953: 385). Either way, there is no denying whilst progressive in other respects, most of Rousseau's comments about Sophie's education may be considered reactionary by today's standards.

Nevertheless, a number of points must be held in mind when studying Rousseau. Firstly, Rousseau's rhetorical style of writing (indeed, in this circumstance, it seems important to recall that *Emile* is a work of fiction) means that he frequently exaggerated matters and agitated the emotions of his readers, which sometimes resulted in statements that he did not fully believe in himself. Secondly, and relevantly, Sophie's education must be understood within the broader context of Rousseau's writings on philosophy, politics, and religion. This is the only way to delineate the core concepts of Rousseau's thought and philosophy. Lastly, *Emile* must be understood within the context of Rousseau's other writings, those of his contemporaries as well as ancient Greek and Roman writers.

As such, by contextualising Rousseau's education for women, the most significant contribution of this dissertation to the current literature concerns clarifying the importance of the 'general will' and social institutions on the way people may be accorded different social and sexual roles within their relationships. In other words, while the concept of love (or the need for an active or passive partner) remains consistent, different societies use differing genderlectical discourses regarding each individual and their subsequent social positions within their specific culture. Put more simply, for Rousseau, Sophie's unique education may only be explained by the way French society was designed in that epoch; that, ultimately, his view of women's education was purely a consequence of the social institutions and history of France. Otherwise, he believed, France could not function ideally, according to the state of its 'general will'.

What that means for Philosophy of Education is that although the core principles propounded in *Emile* might be relevant in all cases, the people who fit into the roles described in the book may vary according to the circumstances of a society and its 'general will'. It goes without saying, this has significant implications for gender studies as well, especially because this way of approach leaves open the possibility of discussing roles various genders can or have to adopt in order to prove their function as model citizens. For instance, in the context of our 'postmodern' days, in which transsexuality has become a burning issue, a number of traditional assumptions are being directly challenged in the sphere of education and beyond. For instance, in Chen-Hayes' 'Counselling and Advocacy With

Transgendered and Gender-Variant Persons in Schools and Families', it is intriguingly observed that non-traditional concepts of gender identity have been ignored or, sadly, pathologised in educational institutions and family counselling settings; each theme is proving to be a highly-fertile topic for future researches. Obviously, although it could be stated that this has fundamental implications on the freedom of individuals in society, this dissertation never attempted to assess Rousseau's view of an ideal society or politics. As alluded to in earlier chapters, in fact, it assessed Sophie's education whilst having in mind Rousseau's 'social contract'. All meaning, not surprisingly, the moment we criticise or slightly change Rousseau's broader philosophical and political framework, Sophie's education, or in fact Emile's education, may not hold together.

Everything considered, it is worth remembering that the novel *Emile* was, if examined deeply, intended to educate its readers more than propound an educational system (Schaeffer, 1998: 607). In some ways, then, it could be said that Rousseau, as the author, acted like a 'tutor' to his readers without the audience's knowledge — guiding their thoughts, whilst concurrently leading them towards becoming ideal citizens within their particular society. So, by means of literary expansion, Rousseau undertakes a minimal level of violence towards inherited notions, whereas at the same time manifestly expands the expectations and perceptions of educational narratives amid readerships in the 18th century. For all that, although Rousseau's influence on systems of education is diminishing — perhaps for reasons relating to outdated women's education — it may be worth revisiting some of his ideas in light of the substantial misunderstandings that continue to overshadow his work. As such, it is hoped this thesis has assisted this developmental process.

SECTION II BIBLIOGRAPHY

Aristotle. [340 BC] 1976. *Ethics*. London: Penguin Books.

Barnes, J. 1976. Introduction. In Aristotle, *Ethics*. London: Penguin Books, pp. 9-43.

Butterworth, C. E. 1992. Preface. In J.-J. Rousseau, *The Reveries of the Solitary Walker*. Indianapolis: Hackett Publishing Company, pp. vii-xix.

Chen-Hayes, S. F. 2011. 'Counseling and Advocacy With Transgendered and Gender-Variant Persons in Schools and Families'. *The Journal of Humanistic Counseling, Education and Development* 40 (1), pp. 34-48.

Cohen, J. M. 1953. Introduction. In J.-J. Rousseau, *The Confessions*. London: Penguin Books, pp. 7-14.

Cranston, M. 1968. Introduction. In. J.-J. Rousseau, *The Social Contract*. London. Penguin Books, pp. 9-43.

Darling, J. 1994. *Child-Centered Education and its Critics*. London: Paul Chapman.

Darling, J. & Pijpekamp, M. van de. 1994. 'Rousseau on the education, domination and violation of women'. *British Journal of Educational Studies* 42 (2), pp. 115-132.

Defoe, D. 1993. *Robinson Crusoe*. Ware, Hertfordshire: Wordsworth Classics.

Dent, N. 2005. *Rousseau*. London and New York: Routledge.

France, P. 1987. *Rousseau: Confessions*. Cambridge: Cambridge University Press.

Hanson, V. D. 2009. *Western Ways of War: Infantry Battle in Classical Greece*. Berkeley: University of California Press.

Homer. [762 BC] 1966. *The Iliad*. Harmondsworth, Middlesex: Penguin Books.

Jimack, P. D. 1974. Introduction. In J.-J. Rousseau, *Emile*. London: Dent, pp. v-xxvi.

Kessen, W. 1978. 'Rousseau's children'. *Rousseau for Our time* 107 (3), pp. 155-166.

Kodelja, Z. 2015. 'The voice of conscience in Rousseau's Emile'. *Ethics and Education* 10 (2), pp. 198-208.

Locke, J. [1693] 1824. *Some Thoughts Concerning Education*. [online]. Available at: http://oll-resources.s3.amazonaws.com/titles/1444/0128-08_Bk.pdf [Accessed 10 September 2019]

Mill, J. S. [1859] 1991. *On Liberty and Other Essays*. Oxford: Oxford University Press.

Munro, A. 2020. 'State of nature'. [online]. *Encyclopædia Britannica*. Available at: https://www.britannica.com/topic/state-of-nature-political-theory [Accessed 26 August 2020]

Parry, D. W. 2011. *Caliban's Redemption*. London: Finatran.

Parry, D. W. 2019. *Mount Athos Inside Me: Essays on Religion, Swedenborg and Arts*. Melbourne: Manticore Press.

Plato. [c. 375 BC] 1974. *The Republic*. Harmondsworth, Middlesex: Penguin Books.

Plato. [c. 399 BC] 1987. *Early Socratic Dialogues*. London: Penguin Books.

Plato. [c. 385–370 BC] 1998. *Symposium*. Oxford: Oxford University Press.

Rousseau, J.-J. [1750] 2008. *Discourse on the Arts and Sciences*. [online]. Available at: https://www.files.ethz.ch/isn/125491/5018_Rousseau_Discourse_on_the_Arts_and_Sciences.pdf [Accessed 12 September 2019]

Rousseau, J.-J. [1983] no date. *Discourse on Inequality*. [online]. Available at: https://aub.edu.lb/fas/cvsp/Documents/DiscourseonInequality.pdf879500092.pdf [Accessed 30 September 2019]

Rousseau, J.-J. [1782] 1953. *The Confessions*. London: Penguin Books.

Rousseau, J.-J. [1762] 1968. *The Social Contract*. London: Penguin Books.

Rousseau, J.-J. [1762] 1974. *Emile*. London: Dent.

Rousseau, J.-J. [1782] 1992. *The Reveries of the Solitary Walker*. Indianapolis: Hackett Publishing Company.

Schaeffer, D. 1998. 'Reconsidering the Role of Sophie in Rousseau's "Emile"'. *Polity* 30 (4), pp. 607-626.

Simons, M. 1990. 'Why Can't a Man Be More Like a Woman? (A Note on John Locke's Educational Thought)'. *Educational Theory* 40 (1), pp. 135-145.

Thomas, P. 1991. 'Jean-Jacques Rousseau, Sexist?'. *Feminist Studies* 17 (2), pp. 195-217.

Waterfield, R. 1998. Introduction. In: Plato, *Symposium*. Oxford: Oxford University Press, pp. xi-xl.

Watt, D. 1987. Introduction. In: Plato, *Early Socratic Dialogues*. London: Penguin Books, pp. 119-127.

Weiss, P. A. 1987. 'Rousseau, Antifeminism, and Woman's Nature'. *Political Theory* 15 (1), pp. 81-98.

Williams, D. L. 2010. 'Rousseau's Platonic Enlightenment'. *Philosophy in Review* 30 (4), pp. 309-311.

Wokler, R. 2001. *Rousseau: A Very Short Introduction*. Oxford: Oxford University Press.

Wollstonecraft, M. [1792] 2017. *A Vindication of the Rights of Woman with Strictures on Political and Moral Subjects*. [online]. Available at: https://www.earlymoderntexts.com/assets/pdfs/wollstonecraft1792.pdf [Accessed 9 March 2019]

AN AFTERWORD ON ANTHROPOSOPHICAL EDUCATION

DAVID WILLIAM PARRY

To my mind, a philosophy of tuition and learning is a simple enough pursuit. After all, any additional examination of the goals, methods, and meaning of educational processes per se are more than welcome in these postmodern times. Especially, perhaps, when handled by the expert palms of eminent scholars like Professor Judith Suissa of the Institute of Education, alongside Daniele-Hadi Irandoost as a fully-qualified teacher, author, and historian. Who, one quickly needs to add, is a surprisingly young man already known for his sensitive and probing exploration of multidisciplinary materials from a series of truly refreshing angles. In which case, my initial engagement with this book from the lazy viewpoint of someone assuming it merely offered an analysis of the themes outlined above, not to mention an inspection of the various pedagogical approaches to mental training, proved woefully inadequate. Furthermore, every reconsideration proved urgent, since they coexisted beside revaluations regarding the manner wherein this profession relates to broader sociocultural contexts as an academic discipline frequently forced to overlap didactic techniques generally with practical philosophies in particular.

Hence, my stock Hegelian standpoint, whereupon institutional 'life forms' interweave through a variety of aesthetic crosscurrents constituting a so-called 'second nature' allowing every human being to participate in the realm of inherited norms revealed by upbringing, as well as bequeathed, sentient, values, very quickly abated. Certainly, instead of predictable and dreary overviews, asphyxiating spreadsheets, or overwhelmingly pedestrian tautologies (usually characteristic of 'educative' fields), I soon discovered essays aiming at something much deeper and far more intriguing. Chapters whereon Irandoost plays with style and content in order to tease previously withheld perspectives from materials otherwise reduced to a decimating boredom. Contrarily then, this vigorous volume attempts to uncover a *Universitas Litterarum*, or in other words, an emergent unity existing between subject, research, and teaching, as a means to enlighten our otherwise entropic predicament.

Thus, my first reading of *On the Philosophy of Education: Towards an Anthroposophical View* immediately demanded a second, more careful, perusal of the text. Especially so, once I had confirmed Irandoost was looking for a genuine revolution in tutelage overall. Furthermore, his appraisals rapidly proved reminiscent of Ivan Illich in the latter's masterpiece *Deschooling Society* as a work placing creativity at the heart of our human condition, while also regarding this primary, anthropic, attribute as spontaneous and intrinsically valuable. Each a radical position, of course, whereby a joke, an idea, a literary endeavour, a musical composition, or a painting, witness the unfolding of previously unsuspected gifts and solutions to congenital heuristic problems. Accompanied, as these shared unveilings usually are, by honestly inventive ways to experience worthwhile personal instruction. Now, as a text divided into two broad segments, it goes without saying, Irandoost speedily displays a prodigious grasp of these erudite topics, whilst listing anarchist alternatives to mainline education, the use of language and 'extended-mind' theory, to say nothing of psychoanalytic strategies used to promote deeper imaginative expression, as adjunct concerns. What is more, his masterful second section scrutinises often-overlooked writings on women's education in *Emile* by Jean–Jacques Rousseau before summarising a nearly hidden egalitarianism towards both traditional genders inside this Swiss-born philosopher's tome. Yet, Irandoost undeniably comes into his own when focusing on a specifically Anthroposophical undercurrent in such affairs, wherefrom profoundly informed conversations involving cognitive science, theology, psycholinguistics, technology, sociology, and even economics, are held as signposts relating to the various manifestations of intelligence altogether. At which point, a number of additional issues organically arise. For example, the relationship between personality type and creative ability, creativity and mental health, the potential for fostering creativity when the latter is clearly augmented by technology, as well as the application of resources to improve the effectiveness of learning and teaching procedures through virtual scenarios, all manifestly beg for a supplementary volume. Either way, an overtly Anthroposophical frame of expectation has suddenly come into our propaedeutic foreground.

To elaborate his stance a little further, Irandoost tentatively dialogues with Anthroposophy as a philosophical stratagem founded during the early 20th century by the renowned Austrian polymath Rudolf Steiner. An extraordinarily accomplished man who postulated the presence of an intellectually comprehensible and objective spiritual world accessible to human experience. As such, Anthroposophy has its roots in German idealist and mystical colleges, whereas Steiner himself defined it as 'a scientific exploration of the spiritual world' even though others have variously named it a 'philosophy and cultural movement', or a 'system of thought'. Therefore, in terms of the philosophy of education, Irandooost is quick to suggest Anthroposophical ideals have been intuitively applied to a string of 'alternative' educational enterprises like Waldorf schooling, as well as the Camphill movement, whereabouts contemporary models akin to 'honing theory' appear employed to maximum effect. Particularly so, when these initiatives posit that creativity emerges from a self-mending, self-organising, worldview. All meaning, a succession of Steiner's contentions imply everyone continually hones (and re-hones) their developmental interaction with the biosphere around them, albeit with different levels of commitment. A stance explaining why Irandoost occasionally hints Anthroposophy (like honing theory itself), continually emphasises externally visible outcomes for internal cognitive restructuring through creative enactment. Unquestionably, this noted, there are times when Irandoost contends the one factor distinguishing Anthroposophical views from other rival models in creative education is their focus on an incessant restructuring as this pertains to any conceptions of a fixed task. Atop such artistries, he indirectly proposes Waldorf teachers recount any allaying of creatively demanding endeavours with scarce educational supplies simply produces a further interaction betwixt conceptions of the job at-hand and their expanding *weltanschauung*. Thereafter, secondary and tertiary conceptions easily adapt through an unswerving interaction with their prevailing hermeneutic *in toto*. What is more, due to Waldorf practitioners affirming creative processes naturally reflect their Anthroposophical paradigms (because they invariably seek internal consistency among a given set of mental components), this, in itself, helps to facilitate repairs required by any rupturing amid a task and its conception. All in all, they liken these cerebral systems to physical bodies seeking their own health-giving renewal. So stated, Irandoost's near-obsession with these fascinating methodologies become instantly apparent.

Still, at the day's end, existence itself is the first cause of every question, along with a settlement to each inquiry. Possibly, this is why there is always something inherently theistic in any discussion referring to the intimacies of reciprocal education, the location and financial impetus of learning as an avowedly socio-conformist activity, as well as those titanic mysteries encountered along the road to any disclosure of our psyche. These are, after all, private and transpersonal issues at the same time. If implicitly granted, however, anyone candidly wishing to revel in theses affecting every one of us individually, quite aside from our families, clan, and nation, *On the Philosophy of Education: Towards an Anthroposophical*

View by Daniele-Hadi Irandoost is on the level of a must-read. A textual delight, dare I contest, reminding its readers that each description of Being remains awash with educational anecdotes and oppositions stretching beyond themselves into something utterly transcendent. Consequently, I do not have the slightest reservation in recommending this remarkable book to our Anglophone audiences as a captivating contribution to the humble art of human betterment.

The Rt Rev'd Dr David William Parry OSB FRAS

London 2022

ACKNOWLEDGEMENTS

I would like to thank the following persons for their support, assistance and inspiration: John Barnwell, Dr Roger Prentis, Neil Watson, Father Alan Cox, Glyn Paflin, and Gwendolyn Taunton for her patience and unfailing belief in this project.

APPENDIX: A METHODOLOGICAL CRITIQUE OF SKINNERS BEHAVIOUR 'SCIENCE'

> My parents were looking for a school that would nurture the whole person. They also felt that the Waldorf school would be a far more open environment for African Americans, and that was focused on educating students with values, as well as the academic tools necessary to be constructive and contributing human beings ... I think the end result of Waldorf education is to raise our consciousness.
> — *Kenneth Chenault, Chairman and CEO of American Express*

There is little doubt Skinner has had noticeable influence on the study of education. Certainly, in this regard, behaviourism is still widely read in core text books (if not training courses) on teaching and learning, amidst such other theories as constructivism and social constructivism as propounded by Piaget and Vygotsky, respectively. Nevertheless, behaviourism has faced persistent and robust criticisms ever since its emergence. The aim of this brief reflection is to assess behaviourism, particularly through an evaluation of the 'methodology' in Skinner's work on behaviour 'science'. Primarily, this is due to the fact theoretical inquiries must be based on suitable scientific methodology first and foremost, especially if one intends to plan or design valid practices in schools. So, divided into three parts, the first sets out Skinner's understanding of behaviourism and details how it may be implemented in teaching and learning. The second, subsequently, examines the methodological weakness found in Skinner's writing. The third part, finally, sketches a point from behaviourism that may still be relevant in educational praxis notwithstanding the counterargument in section two.

Part I: Behaviourism and Skinner

To begin with, behaviourism is advocated on the basis that repetitive external, environmental stimuli determine the actions or behaviour of animals by affecting their in-built program (nature). Inspired by the work of Pavlov on 'conditioned reflexes', Skinner's experiment famously consisted of pigeons, which were taught to act in a certain way depending on the applied external stimuli (Encyclopaedia Britannica, 2019). In one particular experiment, for instance, Skinner's pigeons received food when they turned or pecked depending on the word appearing on the wall (Jenningh, 2007). Through repetition, in this manner, the pigeons learned to follow the instructions of an external factor whenever it showed, and vice versa.

Therefore, when applied to an educational setting, Skinner claimed learning is a direct outcome of repetition around a system of rewards and punishments, as external causes. He believed, in other words, education in its entirety is behaviouristic and children learn best through the reinforcement of rules and regulations for answering questions correctly or wrongly. Unlike theorists who emerged later, effectively, Skinner neglected the significance given to independent-learning or social interaction as different means of learning. Basically, in current terminology, his theory may be perceived as 'teacher-centric', as opposed to 'student-centric', a belief ultimately evident in his contention that there is little or no such thing as 'free will' (Los Angeles Times, 1990).

Part II: A Methodological Weakness

While Skinner still retains some small clout amidst behaviourists today, his ideas have been frequently censured and repudiated. In this respect, perhaps the most famous is Chomsky's review of Skinner's *Verbal Behaviour*. Often cited as the definitive evidence against the adequacy of behaviourism, Chomsky's paper concerns the way Skinner treats behaviourism as a science. For Skinner, it may be said, behaviourism is not only self-evident, but applicable to every other aspect of life, including 'history, sociology, psychology' as Chomsky pointed out (Virués-Ortega, 2006). Consequently, one might add, Skinner's viewpoint was something like 'the study of data', rather than the study of the brain, which is the source of 'competence, capacity' (ibid.).

To develop this point further, Chomsky also noted experiments conducted on animals could not be simply applied to humans *ipso facto*, and that doing so would be unscientific. Specifically, Chomsky argued extending results 'from the animal laboratory to the [human] domain of verbal behaviour might not be justified', but would necessitate exclusive principles altogether (Palmer, 2006). Put simply, Chomsky supposed 'the behaviour of nonverbal organisms' is qualitatively different from 'human verbal behaviour', whilst Skinner thought otherwise (ibid.). Overall, Chomsky confirmed his main criticism was that since Skinner's analysis is false when it is taken literally, it can only be 'intended metaphorically', if not in terms of mere play with words (ibid.). It goes without saying, taking into account the historical development of Skinner's thought, behaviourism lost influence when constructivism (Piaget) and social constructivism (Vygotsky) emerged as major educational theories, later.

Part III: Redeeming Behaviourism and Skinner

Notwithstanding the methodological flaw in Skinner's argument, admittedly, it offers some insight into human behaviour, albeit when one treats it as one theory among other theories. In this manner, drawing upon daily practices in the UK, it is possible to see so-called 'behaviour management' in primary and secondary state schools follow Skinner's conception of punishments and rewards, one way or another, in the form of such things as notes in diary, seclusion, stickers, candies, so on (see, for example, Watergate School, 2018). In this sense, additionally, despite the fact behaviourism does not properly apply to the actual learning of knowledge, it seems to have some utility in relation to 'behaviour management'; that is, of course, to the extent we do not take into account extreme cases (for instance, 'special needs' children).

As such, when treated as one theory among others, behaviourism may be viewed as an addition to theories like social constructivism, which hold, for instance, that behaviour management requires the 'active' involvement of the individual through a transformative internalisation of the 'social, cultural and historical context' (Postholm, 2013: 396); in a way, this might be applied via pupil participation in the making of classroom rules to ensure understanding of their purpose and rationale. As research indicates, however, sometimes it is vital 'teachers enforce rules and that demands are placed on the pupils', in accordance with behaviourism, for effective learning (ibid.). All suggesting, in short, no theory is irrelevant as long as it is not perceived as the sole interpretation.

Conclusion

The case for behaviourism as advocated by Skinner appears difficult to uphold nowadays in view of the criticisms it has confronted over the years from various standpoints. This brief reflection outlined one such criticism regarding an initial, but crucial, flaw in Skinner's methodology. Fundamentally, by pointing to his all-encompassing 'belief' in behaviourism, it indicated how Skinner was scientifically mistaken, if not entirely wrong. On the other hand, it drew attention to the practical applicability of his system of punishments and rewards on 'behaviour management', as repeatedly evidenced in the official policies of primary and secondary state schools in the UK. The important thing to bear in mind, all things considered, is while all theories may have an element of truth, they can never offer an overarching explanation for everything. This is true not only of Skinner's work but of every other theory studied within the academic field of education.

BIBLIOGRAPHY

Encyclopædia Britannica. 2019. *B. F. Skinner*. Available at: https://www.britannica.com/biography/B-F-Skinner [Accessed 29 October 2019].

Jenningh. 2007. Operant conditioning. [online]. Available at: https://www.youtube.com/watch?v=I_ctJqjlrHA [Accessed 29 October 2019].

Los Angeles Times. 1990. B. F. Skinner, 86, Behaviourist and Author Dies. [online]. *Los Angeles Times*. Available at: https://www.latimes.com/archives/la-xpm-1990-08-20-mn-751-story.html [Accessed 29 October 2019].

Palmer, D. C. 2006. 'On Chomsky's Appraisal of Skinner's *Verbal Behaviour*: A Half Century of Misunderstanding'. *Behav Anal* Fall 29 (2), pp. 253-267. Available at: https://www.ncbi.nlm.nih.gov/pmc/articles/PMC2223153/ [Accessed 29 October 2019].

Postholm, M. B. 2013. 'Classroom Management: what does research tell us?'. *European Educational Research Journal* 12 (3), pp. 389-402.

Virués-Ortega, J. 2006. 'The Case Against B. F. Skinner 45 years Later: An Encounter with N. Chomsky'. *Behav Anal* Fall 29 (2), pp. 243-251. Available at: https://www.ncbi.nlm.nih.gov/pmc/articles/PMC2223151/ [Accessed 29 October 2019].

Watergate School. 2018. *Behaviour Management Policy*. Available at: http://www.watergate.lewisham.sch.uk/school-policies/behaviour-management-policy/ [Accessed 29 October 2019].

www.ingramcontent.com/pod-product-compliance
Lightning Source LLC
Chambersburg PA
CBHW032257150426
43195CB00008BA/492